"Author Lisa Schab recognizes that teen clarifies how youths experience many mixeu emotions, thoughts, and feelings as they navigate this time in their lives. Readers are provided with practical exercises and encouraged to explore their findings to develop self-awareness. The book is filled with examples of real-life situations that all teenagers can relate to, and is a useful tool (resource) for teens today."

—**Kristen Dahl, MS,** student counselor at
College of Lake County

"In a culture where value is often measured by how many follow-ers or likes you attain on social media, this book by Lisa Schab hits the mark. It will help readers positively construct a strong knowledge of healthy self-esteem and how to create it. This is a must-read for all teens!"

—**Lucie Hemmen, PhD,** licensed clinical psychologist,
author of *Parenting a Teen Girl* and *The Teen Girl's
Survival Guide,* and mother of two teen girls

"The teen years can be tough on self-esteem, and young people who struggle need practical information they can understand and use right away. Lisa Schab skillfully translates powerful clinical concepts from mental health research and treatment, and offers them to adolescents in plain talk. *Self-Esteem for Teens* is a valuable guide for all youth. These principals work!"

—**Britt H. Rathbone, MSSW, LCSW-C,** expert adolescent
therapist, trainer, author, and coauthor of *What Works
with Teens, Dialectical Behavior Therapy for At-Risk
Adolescents,* and *Parenting a Teen Who Has Intense Emotions*

"This interactive book has a wonderful balance of great advice, fun stories, examples that teenagers can relate to, and practical exercises and strategies that are easy to apply, but powerful. It is insightful, easy to read, and has all the ingredients to help anyone take control of their self-esteem and their life."

—**Nadine Kunesh, MEd, MS**, high school teacher in Carlsbad, CA, and former teacher and parent group program coordinator for Community Home Education Program (CHEP)

"Lisa Schab's book empowers teens to take charge of their self-esteem through the use of stories, exercises, and affirmations. *Self-Esteem for Teens* teaches the reader how to manage their emotions while reminding them that it's okay to make mistakes. Schab's expertise and understanding of the adolescent experience is evident in her writing as she is able to provide practical solutions while also showing compassion for the teenage experience."

—**Emily Hasselquist, LCSW**, high school social worker at Warren Township High School, and therapist in private practice

"*Self-Esteem for Teens* is a rich resource for teens to understand the power they have in thinking positively about themselves. The organization and practical exercises make this book helpful either on its own or as a supplement to therapy."

—**Michael L. Welsh, PsyD**, clinical psychologist and executive director at Cornerstone Family Counseling

"Lisa Schab's new book *Self-Esteem for Teens,* is an innovative guide for young adults, their parents, and helping professionals in developing healthy attitudes and positive self-images. Presented in clear, descriptive writing, this workbook offers a logical approach to delving into six key principles that when put into practice can transform a teen's life. Schab explains brain biology in easily understandable terms, and then how healthy self-esteem puts happiness and success within reach in all aspects of a teen's life: school, social, family, and work situations…. Schab's use of 'wisdom tales' and contemporary examples allows teens to feel good about their individuality as they explore and challenge their thought processes…. This is a powerful workbook that will greatly benefit young people and those who care about them."

> —**Mary Jo Belenski, EdD**, assistant professor and
> undergraduate public health program coordinator
> at Montclair State University

"There are many adolescents who struggle with low self-esteem, and *Self-Esteem for Teens* provides crucial information and tools to help them reach their full potential. Schab's writing is clear yet insightful, providing numerous examples and exercises to engage teens and their parents. Clinicians will find the book highly useful in guiding their clients. In a word—invaluable!"

> —**Jeremy S. Kaplan, MD**, board-certified child,
> adolescent, and adult psychiatrist, and assistant
> professor of psychiatry and behavioral sciences at
> Feinberg School of Medicine, Northwestern University

the *i* n s t a n t   h e l p
s o l u t i o n s   s e r i e s

Young people today need mental health resources more than ever. That's why New Harbinger created the **Instant Help Solutions Series** especially for teens. Written by leading psychologists, physicians, and professionals, these evidence-based self-help books offer practical tips and strategies for dealing with a variety of mental health issues and life challenges teens face, such as depression, anxiety, bullying, eating disorders, trauma, and self-esteem problems.

Studies have shown that young people who learn healthy coping skills early on are better able to navigate problems later in life. Engaging and easy-to-use, these books provide teens with the tools they need to thrive—at home, at school, and on into adulthood.

This series is part of the **New Harbinger Instant Help Books** imprint, founded by renowned child psychologist Lawrence Shapiro. For a complete list of books in this series, visit newharbinger.com.

self-esteem
for teens

six principles
for creating the
life you want

LISA M. SCHAB, LCSW

Instant Help Books
An Imprint of New Harbinger Publications, Inc.

Publisher's Note

This publication is designed to provide accurate and authoritative information in regard to the subject matter covered. It is sold with the understanding that the publisher is not engaged in rendering psychological, financial, legal, or other professional services. If expert assistance or counseling is needed, the services of a competent professional should be sought.

Distributed in Canada by Raincoast Books

Copyright © 2016 by Lisa M. Schab
          Instant Help Books
          An Imprint of New Harbinger Publications, Inc.
          5674 Shattuck Avenue
          Oakland, CA 94609
          www.newharbinger.com

Cover design by Amy Shoup; Acquired by Tesilya Hanauer; Edited by Karen Schader

Library of Congress Cataloging-in-Publication Data on file

Printed in the United States of America

18   17   16

10   9   8   7   6   5   4   3   2   1   First printing

This book is dedicated to those four who were my parents, whose strengths I adopted and whose struggles pushed me to grow and seek new ways; to Nancy S., who so gently and consistently filled in the gaps; and to W., who sat behind my chair.

Contents

Read This First: How Self-Esteem
Can Work for You   1

part 1: core beliefs

wisdom tale: The Town Up Ahead   13

principle 1   My Self-Esteem Is in My Hands   14

wisdom tale: The Queen's Garden   43

principle 2   Every Human Being Has Intrinsic Value
and Worth, Including Me   44

wisdom tale: Three Friends   67

principle 3   My Greatest Value, Potential, and Power
Lie in My Authentic Self   69

part 2: power-filled choices

wisdom tale: The Wolf   99

principle 4   Feeding the Positive Grows the Positive   100

wisdom tale: The Butterfly   119

principle 5   There Is a Reward in Every Struggle   120

wisdom tale: The Donkey   143

principle 6   I Am Not Limited by My Circumstances   144

Ending Note   169

Acknowledgments   171

How Self-Esteem Can Work for You

We all want to feel good about ourselves. We want to wake up in the morning and believe we matter. We want to believe we're loved. We want to believe we have value.

Many of us go through life running after this feeling. We see it as something that might happen in the future—when we get something in particular we want, when someone in our life validates us, when we accomplish a certain goal, or when we finally have the right circumstances. We believe that when something changes, we will finally feel good about ourselves.

The problem with this belief is that it gives away our power. It makes us dependent on other people, certain circumstances, or the future for our happiness. It keeps us running after, but never catching, the good feeling about ourselves we're seeking.

The purpose of this book is to teach you these facts:

- Your true power lies within you.

- The ability to wake up in the morning and believe you matter, are loved, and have value is completely—and only—within your control.

- It's only your mind that needs to change for you to feel good about yourself.

- You can achieve that good feeling right now all by yourself.

- That good feeling is called healthy self-esteem.

What Is Healthy Self-Esteem?

It's important to be clear on what healthy self-esteem really means. If you understand it, you'll realize how important it is, how it affects your entire life, and why putting energy and focus into its development is worth the effort.

Very basically, self-esteem is how you feel about yourself. If you want to feel authentically good about yourself, truthfully, down at the deepest level, you need healthy self-esteem.

People with healthy self-esteem generally have positive thoughts and feelings about themselves. They are certain enough of their equality with others that they can admit their faults without feeling ashamed and enjoy their strengths without putting others down.

People without healthy self-esteem generally have negative thoughts and feelings about themselves. They are not confident in their equality to others, so they feel ashamed when they make mistakes and may put others down in order to cover up their insecurity.

Madeline gets a poor grade on her English paper and tells herself she's stupid. She walks into a party and no one says hi to her, so she tells herself she's a loser. She applies for a job but doesn't get it and tells herself she didn't deserve it anyway.

Madeline generally feels bad about herself. This is an example of unhealthy self-esteem.

Jacob gets a poor grade on his English paper and tells himself he needs to put in more effort next time. When he walks into a party and no one says hi to him, he goes over and says hi to someone himself. He applies for a job but doesn't get it and tells himself he'll try again with another job. Jacob generally feels good about himself. This is an example of healthy self-esteem.

When Sarah hits the winning run in the baseball game, she cheers her success and celebrates the team effort with her fellow players. She treats the coach to pizza and thanks her for her help during the season. She happily displays her trophy in her bedroom. Sarah generally feels good about herself, and her actions are examples of healthy self-esteem.

When Kevin hits the winning run in the baseball game, he cheers his success and talks about how the team couldn't have won without him. He tells the coach to buy him a pizza and name him Most Valuable Player as reward for the victory. He puts his trophy in his locker, showing everyone—but warning them not to touch it. From the outside, it may look as if Kevin feels good about himself, but on the inside he doesn't truly believe in his equality to others. To cover up his insecurity, he acts like he thinks he's really great. He actually needs to overact in order to convince himself. Kevin's actions are examples of unhealthy self-esteem.

Healthy self-esteem is a deep knowing that you are a valuable person and so is everyone else. When you have healthy self-esteem, you don't need to have someone else affirm you or to achieve a certain goal to feel good about yourself. You don't have to feel better than someone else to know you're okay. You know your self-worth doesn't depend on whether you win or lose.

Healthy self-esteem includes these characteristics:

- an overall positive regard for yourself

- an understanding and acceptance of your weaknesses

- a celebration of your strengths

- a realistic belief about your equality to others

Teens who have healthy self-esteem have these abilities:

- They know and accept themselves.

- They practice compassion for themselves and others.

- They act with integrity and self-discipline.

- They use healthy coping skills in their thoughts and actions to meet life challenges.

- They keep a conviction of their unconditional worth despite changing circumstances.

- They choose and stand by their own thoughts, feelings, and behaviors, instead of giving in to pressure from others.

- They remain convinced of, and act with respect for, the worth of others.

Thoughts like these come from healthy self-esteem:

- *I'll just keep trying until I get it.*

- *I can tell she doesn't like me, but that's okay.*

- *I love wearing this shirt even though it's not in style.*

- *It's all right if we disagree.*

- *I didn't win, but even placing is awesome.*

Thoughts like these come from unhealthy self-esteem:

- *I have to make the team so I can prove I'm as good as them.*

- *I feel so stupid when I make mistakes.*

- *They're probably lying; it's hard to trust anyone.*

- *I'm always second best.*

- *I hate this school; everyone's conceited.*

Why You Want Healthy Self-Esteem

Your self-esteem is one of the greatest factors in how you'll experience every aspect of your life, because you bring it with you to every situation—classes, parties, dating relationships, job interviews, the family dinner table. When you bring healthy self-esteem, you have a better chance at success and happiness in everything you do.

School

Healthy self-esteem gives you the confidence to ask for help when you don't understand something in class. It lets you leave a party early to study for a test even if your friends want you to stay. It helps you bounce back after you get a low grade, because you know you're not a failure; you just need to work harder. It gives you the confidence to follow your interests and take steps to achieve your dreams when you think about college or career goals. Healthy self-esteem helps you focus on your achievements instead of your mistakes so that you can keep moving forward on your academic path.

Friends

Healthy self-esteem lets you feel good about yourself whether you're the life of the party or the quiet observer. It gives you the confidence to not attend a party if you just don't like crowds. It gives you the power to stand your ground if friends try to talk you into something that you really don't want to do or that you know will get you in trouble. It helps you relax and enjoy life just by being yourself, without having to use substances to have fun or feel comfortable. It helps you worry less about what you'll do, say, or wear, because your self-worth isn't dependent on what other people think. It allows you to develop true friendships based on authenticity and equality, instead of choosing relationships based on social status. It helps you know that your friends truly like the real you—because that's all you ever try to be.

Dating

Having healthy self-esteem in a dating relationship means you're able to compromise: both you and your partner share decision-making equally. It means you're happy when you're with your partner but you also have independent interests; you're not dependent on being together for your happiness or identity. Healthy self-esteem in a relationship means you don't let your partner pressure you into behaviors you aren't ready for or interested in. It means you listen to and respect your partner and your partner listens to and respects you. There's a sense of balance and equality in a healthy dating relationship; both partners contribute equally—emotionally and physically—to the maintenance of the relationship.

Work

When you bring healthy self-esteem to a job—whether that's for a paycheck, volunteer work, or a project outside school—you bring your best self to that work. You're reliable and responsible and do your work to the best of your ability. You get along with and respect your coworkers and supervisors and ask that they respect you, too. When you have healthy self-esteem in the workplace, you're able to learn from constructive criticism and can see your work performance realistically, not over- or underrating your strengths or weaknesses. With healthy self-esteem, you bring honesty and integrity to your job, and people see you as someone they can trust both in and outside the workplace.

Family

When you bring healthy self-esteem to family relationships, you increase the well-being of your whole family. Healthy self-esteem allows you to accept limits your parents or other elders place on you without feeling disrespected or put down. It helps you stand up for and express your own thoughts and feelings appropriately, showing maturity instead of childishness. Healthy self-esteem helps you let go of resentment and bitterness and tolerate disagreements without turning them into grudges or battles. It lets you see the good in each family member even if you don't always like their behavior. Healthy self-esteem creates respect for different opinions, appropriate and open communication, and safe conflict resolution. It builds bridges instead of walls between family members.

How This Book Can Help You Develop Healthy Self-Esteem

You already believe something about yourself and your worth. You already choose thoughts and actions that create good or bad feelings about yourself. The purpose of this book is to teach you specific thoughts and actions that will create healthy self-esteem. These thoughts and actions are presented through six principles that include three core beliefs and three groups of power-filled choices.

Part 1 teaches principles 1, 2, and 3 in the form of core beliefs that are the foundation for taking charge of your self-esteem, truly understanding your value on this planet, and knowing that the best person you can possibly be is yourself. When these beliefs are your inner anchors, you bring them to every situation you encounter, and they give you the power to make behavior choices that will continue to develop and sustain healthy self-esteem.

Part 2 teaches principles 4, 5, and 6 in the form of power-filled choices that create positive experiences in every area of your life. The success these choices bring will help you develop, grow, and maintain an unwavering healthy self-esteem.

Concepts described under each principle are divided into four sections:

- *Learn* gives an explanation of the concept. Read this section to understand the idea that's being presented.

- *Explore* provides exercises for discovering your personal connection to the concept. Complete as many as you like to learn about yourself.

- *Become* provides exercises for making positive changes around this concept. Completing these will help you start creating healthy self-esteem.

- *Affirm* gives statements to help your brain claim the concept. The more you repeat these affirmations, the more the principles of healthy self-esteem will be a part of your thinking and the more empowered you will be.

As you complete any of the exercises, try to observe your answers with an open and curious mind. If you find you're judging yourself, just make an objective mental note of that behavior. Remember, there are no right or wrong answers. The purpose of everything in this book is simply to feed your personal growth.

Since many of the exercises ask you to write an answer or make a list, you'll need separate paper to complete them. It can be helpful to keep all your answers in one place, like a paper or electronic journal. Writing down the answers helps your brain both learn the concept and make the changes you want more quickly.

There are also a number of exercises using visualization, or imagining something that you'd like to accomplish. This may be new to you, but give it a try. Visualization helps make changes in your brain that pave the way for real-life success. This technique is used by many successful athletes, actors, and businesspeople.

Finally, as you travel through this book, keep in mind these suggestions to help you succeed:

- Make progress, not perfection, your goal.

- At any moment, know that wherever you are on your path is exactly where you're supposed to be.

- Be gentle with yourself. There are many tough life circumstances that make it difficult to put new thoughts and actions into place. Allow yourself time, understanding, and any emotions that arise.

- It's an act of wisdom and maturity to ask for help when you need it. Find an adult you trust to give you some support or guidance in hard times.

- Take breaks, but don't give up.

- Relax and enjoy the ride!

part 1

core beliefs

When we believe in something, it means we accept it as true. If you believe in the Tooth Fairy, you tell yourself it's true that when you lose a tooth and put it under your pillow, a tiny fairy will swoop into your room while you're sleeping, pick up the tooth, and leave you a gift in its place. If you believe the earth revolves around the sun, you tell yourself it's true that our planet is in orbit around the nearest star. If you believe your algebra teacher is a fair grader, you tell yourself it's true the grade he gives you accurately reflects your work.

Beliefs are powerful. They directly affect our feelings and behaviors, and so, the course of our lives. Most of the choices we make every day are the result of our beliefs, whether we're conscious of it or not. When you choose a bagel over a donut, it might stem from the belief that a bagel is better for you, or the belief that you'll like the taste better. This choice could affect your health and happiness for the rest of the morning. If you choose to take earth science instead of oceanography, it might stem from the belief that you'll enjoy the subject more, or maybe from the belief that it will be easier. This choice could affect your ability to stay awake in class, your grade point average, or even your choice of college.

Your beliefs about yourself create your self-esteem. Your self-esteem influences the choices you make. The choices you make shape your life.

Garret believes he's a loser. He tells himself it's true he can't achieve his goals, so he chooses not to try because he thinks he'll just fail anyway.

Brooke believes she's inferior to other kids at school. She tells herself it's true she's somehow second-rate, so she chooses to isolate herself and doesn't reach out to make friends because she thinks she'll be rejected.

Adam believes he has equal value to everyone else and a chance at succeeding in most things he tries. He tells himself he's inherently just as good as, but not superior to, other people, and if he doesn't succeed at one thing, he'll try something else. Adam chooses to seek out new friendships and take steps to reach his goals. When the results are positive, he enjoys them; when they're not, he chooses to try again or move on.

The three core beliefs presented in this section are beliefs that underlie healthy self-esteem. When you understand and embrace them, your choices will reflect them, and your life path will be created from a foundation of healthy self-esteem.

The Town Up Ahead

One day, a traveler pulled into a gas station in the countryside and asked the attendant, "What are the people like in the town up ahead?" The attendant replied, "What were the people like in the town you just left?" "Oh," replied the traveler, "they were awful. Rude, cold, unfriendly, hostile. They wouldn't give me the time of day." "I'm sorry to tell you," said the attendant, "but you're going to find the same sort of people in the town up ahead."

A little while later, a second traveler driving in the same direction pulled into the same gas station and asked the same question. "Excuse me," the traveler said, "could you tell me what the people are like in the town up ahead?" "Well," said the attendant, "what were the people like in the town you just left?" "Oh, they were wonderful," the traveler said. "Warm, friendly, kind, patient. Went out of their way to help a stranger." The attendant said, "I'm happy to tell you you're going to find the same kind of people in the town up ahead."

People mistakenly think things are inherently good or bad. More truthfully, things are what we perceive them to be. What we think determines how we experience everything in life, including ourselves.

principle 1

My Self-Esteem Is in My Hands

Many teens mistakenly believe they don't have control over their own self-esteem. They think things like *My brother is so much smarter than me—I can't have healthy self-esteem* or *My coach doesn't play me every game—I can't feel good about myself* or *The person I was dating dropped me for someone else—I'm clearly a loser.*

If our core belief is that someone else or outer circumstances control our self-esteem, we'll be right—these things will control how we feel about ourselves. And we'll never have healthy self-esteem.

If, however, our core belief is that our self-esteem is in our hands, we can always choose to feel good about ourselves no matter what's going on outside of us. We'll gain the benefits of healthy self-esteem, and our thoughts will sound more like these:

- *My brother is so much smarter than me—but I'm creative; we both have valuable strengths.*

- *My coach doesn't play me every game—but if it's important enough, I'll ask her how I can improve so that I can play more.*

- *The person I was dating dropped me for someone else—
  I'm disappointed, but I'll feel better with time, and I'll meet
  someone else, too.*

When we understand that our self-esteem is in our hands,
we're empowered. We're in control of what we think and feel
about ourselves, not other people. We can choose to have healthy
self-esteem in every situation—with family, friendships, dating,
school, and work.

Your Self-Esteem Comes from Your Thoughts

It's not just a nice idea. Your self-esteem *is* in your hands. It comes
from how you think about yourself—and how you think about
yourself is completely up to you. No one else can decide which
thoughts you hold on to. No one else can make you believe anything you don't want to believe. So no one else controls your
self-esteem.

It's true other people can tell you their opinions. They can
share ideas, information, and beliefs. But other people's thoughts
don't automatically become yours unless you choose to let them.

For example, imagine you just got a haircut and you don't
like it. Your friend tells you she thinks it looks great. Does that
mean you automatically think it's great, too? No. You might consider what she says and then change your mind, thinking instead
the haircut isn't that bad. Choosing that thought can make you
dislike it less or even start to like it a lot. However, you could also
hear your friend's opinion, consider it, and decide that no matter
what she says you still don't like your haircut.

Other people can tell us their opinions, but they can't tell us what to think. Only we can decide what we will think.

Jonna was diagnosed with attention deficit/hyperactivity disorder, or ADHD. This means the way her brain works makes it harder for her to focus on certain things. Jonna's cousin, Richie, says, "That's weird. I don't know anyone who has that. You're going to have a hard time in school—and in everything!" Jonna could listen to what Richie says and think, He's right, I'm weird. I'll probably lose my friends when they find out. I might not pass my classes either; it'll be so embarrassing. How can I face people? *Or she could listen to what Richie says and think,* Richie doesn't know much about ADHD; it's a pretty common disorder. I'll need some help at first, but lots of people need help with things. It doesn't make me weird. *Richie can't choose Jonna's thoughts for her. Only Jonna can decide what she thinks.*

Steven plays volleyball on a city league. He wasn't very skilled at the start of the season, but he practiced a lot and improved. His original coach was encouraging and happy with his progress. He told Steven he was becoming an asset to the team and hoped he signed up again. This season, the team has a new coach. He isn't as happy with Steven's skills and never thinks he plays well enough. Steven could recall his first coach and think, I'm doing well and the team values me. *He could listen to the second coach and think,* I don't play as well as I should. *He could also think,* I've improved a lot and can still improve more. *No matter what anyone else says, only Steven can decide what he'll think about his skills.*

Many thoughts arise spontaneously in our minds, but we can choose which ones we value and pay attention to. Because we are each in charge of making this choice with our own thoughts, and our self-esteem comes from how we think about ourselves, we're each in control of our own self-esteem. Your self-esteem is in your hands.

Where Our Thoughts About Ourselves Come From

Where do thoughts of self-like or self-dislike come from? We're not born with thoughts in our heads telling us we like ourselves or we don't. How we think about ourselves comes from a combination of factors:

- brain biology
- family messages
- social messages
- self-messages

When you understand these factors and relate them to your own life, you can learn how to take charge of your self-esteem.

Brain Biology

We're all created with a unique body chemistry. Human beings are like snowflakes—no two are exactly alike. Our physical, emotional, and spiritual selves exist in the form they do as a result of what happened when the DNA from our mothers and fathers combined. Our parents' DNA was a result of their parents' union, and their parents' before them.

Learn

The organ in our body called the brain is like our motherboard. The cells (neurons) and chemicals (neurotransmitters) that make up our brain and decide how it functions are in great part determined by what we inherited from our ancestors. The way our brain works can affect our self-esteem. So everyone's self-esteem is partly the product of biology and genetics.

Different systems, or areas, of our brain can affect self-esteem in different ways:

- The *deep limbic system* sets our emotional tone. It affects our ability to see things in a positive light. When this system is working too hard, we tend to be negatively focused. Too many negative self-thoughts make us dislike ourselves.

- The *basal ganglia* affect anxiety and nervousness. Extreme activity here can create false feelings of being judged or scrutinized. If we think others are criticizing us, we may feel bad about ourselves.

- The *prefrontal cortex* regulates attention and organizational skills. If we have a hard time focusing, we may have a hard time achieving goals. This can bring up feelings of disappointment in ourselves or cause us to think we're failures.

- The *cingulate cortex* affects flexibility and cooperation. These two qualities influence how we handle change and get along with other people. This system can impact our ability to manage day-to-day changes and the quality of our relationships with both others and ourselves. If we struggle to succeed in these areas, we may feel bad about ourselves.

- The *temporal lobes* affect memory, emotional stability, and aggression. Focusing on negative or positive past experiences affects choices we make today. Our emotional stability and aggression level either hinder or help us, since how we act on emotion creates positive or negative feelings about ourselves.

Overly high or low activity in any brain area can affect our behavior. If we do or don't like our behavior choices, we'll feel either good or bad about ourselves.

Our brain systems function with the help of chemicals. The amount of these chemicals and their movement patterns affect our moods, perceptions, and behaviors. For example, serotonin contributes to well-being and happiness; dopamine is associated with the brain's reward system and provides motivation; and norepinephrine impacts attention and focus.

Overly low or high neurotransmitter levels can increase feelings of sadness or anxiety. These feelings can affect our ability to choose positive thoughts about ourselves.

Sonia's mom does yoga and practices mindfulness to manage depression. Sonia's grandfather takes medication to stabilize mood swings. Sonia often finds it hard to think positively. She notices that her first thoughts about any challenge are negative. Her thoughts about herself are mostly negative, too. Sonia gets mad at herself for not being happier. She sees her friends enjoying life more and wonders why she can't relax and have fun. The school psychologist said that because of her family history Sonia could be susceptible to depression. She might have lower serotonin levels or an overactive deep limbic system. Sonia repeatedly practices thinking skills to help shift her brain patterns, changing her automatic thoughts from negative to positive.

Jordan's grandmother and his uncle Max have both been described as "worrywarts." They are both easily stressed, sometimes about very small things. Jordan's dad teases and says they're "as jumpy as ping-pong balls." Both of them have learned to manage their high tension levels by practicing deep breathing and exercising. Jordan's grandmother likes biking and swimming; Uncle Max plays basketball and volleyball. Jordan notices he gets stressed easily, too. He often feels anxious and worries about things that never happen. He notices that when he works out at the gym he's calmer. Jordan's mother explained that he has high anxiety in his genes but physical exercise can help reduce the chemicals that cause it.

When Sonia and Jordan understand their family histories, they realize there's nothing "wrong" with them; they can learn to manage their emotions and feel good about themselves. Your self-esteem is impacted by your physical makeup, but research shows that brains are "plastic"—the chemicals and patterns can change and grow as long as we live. This means you can consciously train your brain to move from negative to positive thoughts and create healthy self-esteem.

We are not victims of our neurons or genes.

—Joanna Holsten

Explore

Investigating your family history can help you understand the brain biology you've inherited. Complete these exercises on separate paper or in your journal.

- Make a list of all your family members. Next to each person's name, write down the personality characteristics that remind you of them. Then do the same for yourself. Add more words if you'd like.

anxious	confident
optimistic	shy
extroverted	pessimistic
fearful	moody
calm	laid-back
aggressive	happy
rebellious	brave
perfectionist	high-strung
addicted	free-spirited
compulsive	depressed

- Review what you've recorded, and list the traits that run in your family. Notice traits of yours that might be genetically based. Tell how it feels to discover this.

- Describe how your inherited brain chemistry might contribute to your healthy or unhealthy self-esteem.

Become

You can affect the chemicals and neural patterns in your brain to create healthier self-esteem. Mindfulness exercises can help. Mindfulness means paying attention without judgment. Mindfulness meditation is a simple exercise you can practice formally, in a quiet place by yourself, or informally, at any time or place. Both ways train your brain to leave distraction, or negative thoughts, and come back to focus, or positive thoughts.

Formal mindfulness

Formal mindfulness gives your brain specific practice time on focusing. Follow these steps:

1. Sit comfortably where you won't be distracted. This spot could be your bedroom, backyard, or any place you can relax quietly.

2. Choose a peaceful object of focus. Some people like nature, such as the image of a sunset, a mountain, or ocean waves. Some choose religious symbols. Some focus on the breath moving in and out of their body. Others like calming words such as "relax," "serenity," or "let go." Experiment to find the focus that feels best for you.

3. Set a timer. Start with one or two minutes. Later, increase little by little, working up to twenty minutes—but take your time. This goal can take months or years to meet.

4. Close your eyes. (If this feels uncomfortable, just gaze downward.)

5. Focus on your peaceful object—your mental image, words, or breath.

6. Accept that your mind will wander—there is no way to prevent this! When your mind wanders, simply notice it without judgment.

7. Refocus on your object of peace.

8. Repeat steps 5–7 until your time is up.

It's critical to remember that mind wandering is not only normal, it's an important part of the practice! Bringing your mind back to your peaceful object over and over is how your brain develops and strengthens its ability to focus. You'll use that ability to leave negative thoughts and return to positive thoughts as you build healthy self-esteem.

Informal mindfulness

Informal mindfulness also involves paying attention without judgment. But instead of sitting alone quietly, you can do it in any circumstances. Follow these steps:

1. At any moment of the day, bring your mind fully to what you're doing. If you're talking with a friend, put all your attention on that friend and what's being said. If you're brushing your teeth, put all your attention on the taste of the toothpaste, the feel of the brush, the motion of your hand. If you're playing a game, notice the hardness of the chair, the colors of the board, the sound of the game pieces moving.

2. As you focus, do so without judgment. Simply be present and observe.

3. Notice without judgment when your mind wanders—as it will!—to the past or future.

4. Come back to focus on the present moment.

5. Repeat steps 1–4 periodically throughout the day.

Like formal practice, informal practice strengthens your brain's ability to leave thoughts you don't want and move to thoughts you do want in order to build healthy self-esteem. The more you practice, the easier it gets.

Affirm

I can train my brain to move toward the positive and create healthy self-esteem.

Family Messages

As soon as a baby is born, it begins hearing messages about itself. Mom says, "Ooh, isn't he cute?" Dad says, "She's got my eyes!" Auntie says, "My, he's a little ball of energy." Grandpa says, "She's going to be an artist!" As we grow, we hear more messages from our family—some repeated over and over.

Learn

Many messages stick with us for a long time, while others are quickly forgotten. The messages we receive from parents and guardians are usually the most significant. As children we're completely dependent on these people for our survival, both emotionally and physically, and we want their love and approval more than anything. Their comments are powerful and begin to shape how we feel about ourselves.

If we repeatedly hear messages like "He'll never be good at sports," or "She's a natural with languages," or "He's going to be an attorney—he's so persuasive," we store these ideas in our memory, and they help create our self-esteem.

It's important to remember that in most families, messages aren't sent to purposely damage self-esteem; however, that doesn't mean it won't happen, for a variety of reasons:

- Our family members are human and imperfect, just like us. Even if they love us very much, they'll make mistakes and sometimes send messages that aren't healthy.

  Chase's mom had a very difficult time delivering him. She recovered fully and loved her son tremendously. But sometimes when Chase misbehaved she'd lose her temper and yell, "After all I went through to bring you into this world, this is what you do to me?" Chase heard this message many times during his childhood and grew up believing that he'd caused his mom much pain by being born and that he still did. Chase felt guilty about this, and this guilt affected his self-esteem. Although he tried not to, if he accidentally hurt someone, it reinforced his belief he shouldn't have been born because he only brought people pain. Chase's mother never meant for her angry comment to affect Chase this way.

- Family members often don't realize they're sending messages.

  When Lily was six, Aunt Grace took her for a haircut. Lily's hair was very thick and curly. When the stylist asked how she wanted the hair cut, Aunt Grace said with a smile, "Oh my, just see if there's anything you can do with this crazy mop-top!" Lily's aunt thought she was only making a light-hearted joke. But when Lily heard the words, she felt embarrassed and began thinking negatively about her looks. She became very sensitive about her hair, wanting to keep it very short so no one would know she had a "mop-top." Lily remembered her aunt's comments well into her teens and struggled with self-esteem issues around her looks. Aunt Grace never knew how her casual comment affected Lily.

- Even the most positively intended messages may be perceived as negative by the receiver.

  Corey's dad was always trying to motivate her. He'd never been encouraged by his own parents and wanted to do better for Corey. Whenever Corey accomplished something, her dad would praise her and then say, "Now let's see if you can do even better next time!" Corey's dad was proud of himself for trying to instill drive and hope into his daughter. But Corey didn't hear his message that way. She grew up thinking she was never good enough because, no matter how much she accomplished, her dad always wanted more. Corey's understanding of her dad's message was very different from what he intended.

When we're very young, our brain can't comprehend the impact these messages have on us. Sometimes we're not even aware of them; they're just part of our lives. Since they're coming from people we're dependent on, and since we're not conscious of their effect, we don't stop to question them. We unconsciously absorb their negative or positive meaning, and this becomes part of how we think about ourselves—our developing self-esteem.

Jillian was always encouraged to conquer her fears. When she was afraid of climbing on the playground bars, her father would hold her carefully and let her take small, cautious steps. He'd say, "Be careful, but give it a try. You can conquer your fears." Later, he would tell her the same thing about trying a new sport or a harder class in school. Jillian heard "You can conquer your fears" over and over until it became an automatic thought. Jillian's self-esteem was shaped by this message, and she grew to be a woman of courage and self-confidence.

Juan was raised by a single mom who was afraid of the unknown and of being hurt physically and emotionally. When she watched Juan on the playground, she often said, "Don't go up there— you might fall!" or "I wouldn't try that if I were you!" or "Juan, you're going to hurt yourself!" Juan heard this about his social and academic life as well. His mom didn't want to see him hurt, so she didn't encourage him to try anything that wasn't a "sure thing." Juan's self-esteem was shaped by these messages, and he grew into a man who was afraid to take risks for fear of failing or being hurt.

Never allow yourself to be made a victim. Accept no one's definition of your life, but define yourself.

—Harvey Fierstein

Explore

The goal of exploring family messages isn't to find someone to blame or credit. Judgment, one way or the other, isn't functional, doesn't contribute to healthy self-esteem, and only gives away your power. The goal is to understand yourself. Complete these exercises on separate paper or in your journal.

- Copy any of the messages you heard as a child or that you still hear today, and add any more you remember. Then tell how each message affected your self-esteem.

  "You're not trying hard enough."

  "You're not good enough."

  "I know you can do this; don't give up."

  "You're driving me crazy."

  "You have talent for that."

  "You're going to be very successful someday."

  "Can't you do anything right?"

  "You're getting stronger and smarter every day."

  "I'm proud of you."

  "Are you stupid or something?"

  "How will you ever get anywhere in life?"

  "I love you just the way you are."

- Write the names of your closest family members or people who lived in your house when you were growing up. These could be parents, guardians, siblings, grandparents, aunts and uncles, cousins, friends, or acquaintances. Next to each name, record the messages that person spoke or still speaks to you. Label each message with a "P" if it affected your self-esteem positively and an "N" if it affected your self-esteem negatively.

- Identify the strongest positive and negative messages you've received or still receive. Explain why your family members may have sent you these messages.

Become

You can consciously change negative messages to positive ones and build healthy self-esteem. Complete these exercises on separate paper or in your journal.

- Choose which of the messages you wrote down you'd like to keep and which you'd like to discard. Rewrite them under the headings "Keep" and "Eliminate."

- Save your "Keep" list. Then use your "Eliminate" list in a powerful way by rewriting every negative message to make it positive. For example, change "You'll never amount to anything" to "I've got great success in my future." Add these new positive messages to your "Keep" list.

- Tell your brain you're ready to think differently by physically destroying your negative messages. Use the following suggestions, or come up with your own—as long as they're safe and appropriate. As you're destroying each message, tell yourself (silently or out loud) that you are removing this message from your life.

- Rip it up and throw it in the garbage.
- Put it through a shredder.
- Cut it up and throw it away.
- Use whiteout to block it out.
- Use a large black marker to obliterate it.
- Type it and delete it.
- Write it on bath tissue and flush it away.

- Remember, no one else can decide your thoughts for you. In the days ahead, reread your "Keep" list and continue feeding yourself these new positive messages. Your self-esteem is in your hands.

Affirm

I can let go of family messages that don't build healthy self-esteem.

Social Messages

We receive messages from the society we live in. They come through media such as radio, television, the Internet, newspapers, movies, and magazines; and from parents, politicians, teachers, faith leaders, writers, lobbyists, experts, business spokespeople, and celebrities.

Learn

Social messages reflect the values of the organization or person sending the message. They usually try to tell us what is "right" and "wrong" according to their beliefs. Social messages try to influence people on how to think, act, or both, in the way they believe is in the best interest of society. It's common to hear social messages about these topics:

education	international relations
politics	minority rights
sexuality	welfare
animal rights	religion
violence	substance abuse
health	science and ethics
safety	the environment
human rights	consumerism
unemployment	aging
economics	children's rights
mental illness	physical attractiveness

We learn social messages when people talk directly to us; for example, when a representative from the Environmental Protection Agency speaks about recycling at a school assembly or in history class when our teacher educates us about civil rights. When our parents tell us they expect us to be honest and reliable, they're directly passing on social values they believe in.

We also learn social messages indirectly. Television commercials for organizations that help prevent child abuse, magazine headlines proclaiming the "best" way to look, and highway billboards promoting certain religious beliefs are all examples of social messages.

Social messages affect our self-esteem by influencing how we feel about ourselves when we do or don't follow social guidelines or fit into the social "norm." Many people are strongly influenced by social messages and feel bad about themselves when they don't measure up to social standards. Many people feel good about themselves when part of their life or themselves matches the social standards in one way or another.

It's important to remember that we have a choice whether we want to agree with social messages. And we have a choice of how we want to feel about ourselves at every moment.

Timothy grew up watching sports with his dad. He memorized all the players' names, their positions, and even personal information about them. Sometimes Timothy and his dad went to sporting events or ate at restaurants owned by famous athletes. Timothy learned indirectly that athletes were revered by his society. In middle school, he wanted to play sports but wasn't very coordinated, and even gym class was hard for him. In high school, Timothy excelled in music and computer science, and he had a solid group of friends. But he always felt bad about himself because he wasn't athletic. Timothy never attended school sporting events because they reminded him he couldn't make the team. He held himself up to the social message that "being athletic is good" and always fell short. Even though he had many other talents and skills, Timothy's self-esteem was low because of what he told himself about sports.

Carly went to a private high school with a strong emphasis on academics. Most of the students planned to go to college and graduate school. Carly got excellent grades but knew she didn't want an advanced degree. What she wanted was to follow in her grandmother's footsteps and weave. Her grandmother had her own loom and made beautiful rugs, blankets, and wall hangings. She had taught Carly to weave when she was little, and Carly already designed her own patterns and exhibited them at art fairs. Some of her classmates thought Carly was crazy and told her she could never make a living that way. Her counselor and teachers advised her to find another skill that was "more marketable in today's society." But Carly knew in her heart that she was going to be a weaver, and she was proud of her talent. She let the other kids laugh, but their opinions didn't affect her self-esteem.

Both Timothy's and Carly's self-esteem is in their own hands, not based on social messages or outer circumstances. They both have choices in what they tell themselves about their differences from the social norm.

Timothy tells himself it's a negative reflection on him that he doesn't have a skill valued by his society. He thinks less of himself because he doesn't meet this social value. Timothy's self-esteem is negatively affected because of the way he thinks of himself in relation to this social message.

Carly tells herself it's not a negative reflection on her that she doesn't want to achieve the things valued by her peers. She doesn't think any less of herself because she doesn't meet this social value. Carly's self-esteem stays healthy because of the way she thinks of herself in relation to this social message.

33

No one can make you feel inferior without your consent.

—Eleanor Roosevelt

Explore

When you're aware of how social messages affect you, you can make choices to maintain healthy self-esteem. Complete these exercises on separate paper or in your journal.

- Make a list of television shows you remember watching as a child and shows you watch now. Identify the social messages you learned from these shows. What did you hear about what society valued? What did you hear about the "best" way to look or dress? What did you hear about the "best" way to live? How did these messages influence your self-esteem as a child? How do they influence your self-esteem now?

- Choose from the subjects below and describe what society tells you about these topics.

minority rights	health
wealth	religion
violence	technology
education	street drugs
sex	food
divorce	marriage

- Rate each subject above from 1 (low) to 10 (high) as to how much you feel you're influenced by these messages. Identify the source or sources from which you receive them; for example, radio, TV, the Internet, printed materials, speakers.

Become

As a teen, you're developing your own values and beliefs, and your self-esteem will be affected by how you choose to express them. Complete the following exercises on separate paper or in your journal.

- Describe your personal beliefs about some of the topics listed above, whether or not they're the same as society's beliefs. Explain why you hold these beliefs.

- Make a list of messages you would want to send viewers if you created a television show or movie that expressed your personal social values. How would you get these messages across?

- List the social values you feel most strongly about. Explain how you can live out these values in a healthy and appropriate way in your daily life.

Affirm

I have a choice about which social messages I believe.

Self-Messages

Perhaps the greatest number of messages we receive comes from ourselves. Whether we realize it or not, we're almost continually "talking to ourselves"—keeping up a running internal chatter from moment to moment. For example, what are you telling yourself right now? *I don't talk to myself... I wish I were outside running... I have to study for geometry... I'm hungry for pizza... I wonder if she'll call me back... I dreamed about cars last night... I hope I have enough money for lunch...*

Every day we hear thousands of self-messages. We tell ourselves judgments, observations, questions, reminders, ideas about things we see and experience, people we know or don't know, and things that happened in the past, may happen in the future, or are happening right now.

Learn

When the messages in our minds are about ourselves, they affect our self-esteem in one way or another. Positive self-messages create healthy self-esteem. Negative self-messages create unhealthy self-esteem.

We may have general self-messages that have been with us for years:

- *I'm a loser.*

- *I'm a good storyteller.*

- *I'm so loved.*

- *I'm a burden.*

We may also have self-messages that are specific to the present moment:

- *I did much better this time.*

- *I shouldn't have said that.*

- *I feel great after that workout.*

- *I'm so embarrassed, I wish I could disappear.*

Self-messages that create healthy self-esteem communicate these qualities:

- self-respect

- self-acceptance

- compassion

- kindness

- forgiveness

- realistic expectations

- healthy self-discipline

These messages might sound like:

- *I forgot my history book; I can borrow my sister's next hour.*

- *He looked right past me; he must not have seen me wave.*

- *I'm feeling really sad; I'm going to call my best friend.*

- *I messed up this time; I'll just give it another try.*

- *My face is breaking out; guess I'll try to smile bigger today!*

- *I'm feeling overwhelmed; I think I'll take a break.*

Self-messages that create unhealthy self-esteem communicate these qualities:

- disrespect

- impatience

- rudeness

- harsh judgment

- condemnation

- unrealistic expectations

- shame

These messages might sound like:

- *I forgot my history book; I'm such an idiot.*

- *He looked right past me; he must hate me.*

- *I'm feeling really sad; I'm such a wimp.*

- *I messed up this time; I'll never get it right.*

- *My face is breaking out; I'm so ugly.*

- *I'm feeling overwhelmed; it figures I couldn't keep up. I'm just no good.*

Jimena wants to be part of her school's color guard. Tryouts are in two weeks, and she's attending practice clinics after school. As much as Jimena wants to be on the squad, she isn't picking up the flag and dance techniques quickly. She gets mad at herself but refuses help from the older members who offer it because she feels embarrassed and thinks they'll laugh at her. Instead of getting the extra training she needs, she leaves the clinic early and berates herself all the way home, telling herself she's so clumsy and awkward she'll never make the squad. She attends one more clinic and then quits, figuring she doesn't have a chance anyway.

Riley is also trying out for color guard. She has a petite build and has never been athletic, so she's struggling to carry the equipment and learn the dance moves. Sometimes she feels discouraged watching other girls pick up both the flags and the routines more easily, but she tells herself that with a little extra practice she can learn what she needs to and do well. When an older member of the color guard offers to help her, Riley says, "Yes, thank you so much!" She gets extra help, practices at home, tries out, and earns a place on the squad.

Both Jimena and Riley sent themselves messages about their ability to learn the tryout routines. Jimena's self-messages were disrespectful and shaming. She didn't achieve her goal and ended up feeling bad about herself. Riley's self-messages were compassionate and forgiving. She achieved her goal and ended up feeling good about herself.

When we talk to ourselves kindly and with acceptance, we're encouraging ourselves and building healthy self-esteem. When we talk to ourselves rudely or with shaming words, we're emotionally abusing ourselves and creating unhealthy self-esteem. As with all other messages, it's important to remember we have a choice.

Your self-esteem is in your hands—nobody is going to hand it to you.

—Yvette Langmaid-Buttery

Explore

When you choose positive self-messages, you're building your own healthy self-esteem. Complete these exercises on separate paper or in your journal.

- What messages do you send yourself in these circumstances?

  - You receive a low grade on a test.
  - Your date stands you up.
  - Your body is bigger or smaller than you'd like it to be.
  - You're not the best player on the team.
  - You forget the beginning of your oral presentation.
  - You trip in the hallway at school.

- How does each of these messages affect your self-esteem?

- As you go through the next few days, pay attention to and record the self-messages running through your head. Count how many contribute to healthy self-esteem and how many do the opposite. How do these two numbers compare?

Become

It's important to remember that all your messages have been learned. And because they were learned, they can also be unlearned. Complete these exercises on separate paper or in your journal.

- Rewrite any negative self-messages you identified above. For example, if your negative message is "Everyone thinks I'm stupid," rewrite it as "I know people who believe in me—including myself."

- Think about how you want to feel about yourself. Then write new self-messages that feed healthy self-esteem. For example:

  "I am capable of great things."

  "I see mistakes as opportunities.

  "I don't have to be perfect to like myself."

  "I accept my vulnerabilities and celebrate my strengths."

  "I'm not superior or inferior to anyone else."

- Sink your healthy self-esteem messages into your subconscious by feeding yourself over and over from your positive thought collection. Use these suggestions or create other ways:

  - Use them as the wallpaper or screen saver on your computer.

  - Set an alarm on your phone so that a healthy message appears at different times during the week.

  - Stick them in your locker, on your dashboard, on your bathroom mirror, or anywhere else you'll see and remember them.

- Put them in your wallet or purse to read when you're feeling down on yourself.

- Send yourself a healthy message in a text or e-mail.

- Keep a healthy message list next to your bed to read when you first wake up and/or before you go to sleep.

- Record the messages on a voice recorder, and play them to yourself on a regular basis.

- Write them on your calendar so that you come across them in the future.

- Write them in your assignment notebook.

Affirm

I choose positive self-messages that create healthy self-esteem.

The Queen's Garden

The queen's garden was vast and stretched for as far as the eye could see. Roses, daffodils, delphinium, daisies, hydrangeas, poppies, nasturtiums, lilies, crocuses, hyacinth, zinnias, irises, peonies, and more. Flowers in each color of the rainbow with petals of every shape and size. One sunny morning, they began conversing among themselves about which of them was the most valuable.

"It must be the rose," said the crocus. "Her petals are like velvet."

"It must be the iris," said the daisy. "Her stature is regal."

"It must be the hyacinth," said the zinnia. "Her fragrance is like heaven."

The flowers couldn't decide, so when the queen came to walk through the garden, they asked her. "Which of us is most valuable?" they said in unison. "And tell us why."

The queen knelt down, taking in the essence of the flowers. "None of you is more valuable than another," she said. "No characteristic overshadows any other. Each seed from which you sprang carried the same treasure of life energy. You are valuable because you exist. The countryside would be barren without you. Your life enriches the lives of all those around you."

Every Human Being Has Intrinsic Value and Worth, Including Me

We all feel self-doubt sometimes. But some of us feel it all the time. We think everybody's better than us. We think we were just born losers, and if everyone in the world were lined up from "best" to "worst," we'd be at the far worst end. We think there's really something wrong with us at the core of our being because we just can't do anything right.

We can think this. But if we do, we're believing a lie.

Consider where that idea came from. Was there a scientific research study that verified we're truly worthless? Did a doctor do a medical test that proved we're flawed? Or is this simply a message we tell ourselves? (If it's a self-message, could we change it?)

Teens who believe they're not as good as their classmates, their friends, or anyone else might have thoughts like these:

- *I'm not like everyone else—I don't belong on this planet.*

- *I just don't fit in—anywhere.*

- *It's like everyone else is winning at a game and I don't even know the rules.*

Everyone has experiences of self-doubt, but when we really understand and believe we all arrive in this world with an equal amount of value and worth, our thoughts sound more like these:

- *Sometimes I think I don't belong on this planet—but it's usually because I'm feeling discouraged about something. I know it's not true and the feeling will pass.*

- *Right now I feel like I don't fit in anywhere—I'm going to call my best friend; he reminds me he's always got my back.*

- *Some days it seems like everyone else is winning at a game I don't even know the rules to—that's when it's time to remember my intrinsic human worth so that I can get my self-esteem back on track.*

The Truth About Human Worth

We've already talked about the power of our thoughts. It's important to remember that holding on to certain thoughts doesn't automatically make them true. For example, we can choose to believe the moon is made of green cheese, but that doesn't make it true. We can choose to believe babies are brought by storks, but that doesn't make it true. Likewise, we can choose to believe we're less valuable than other people, or that we're inherently flawed, but that doesn't make it true.

Each and every human on earth—no matter where they live, what language they speak, what they look like, or who their parents are—like every flower in a garden, arrives on this planet with value and worth. There aren't two rooms in the hospital nursery—one for valuable babies and one for worthless babies. We all arrive as miracles. It's only our thoughts that tell us differently.

If you think you have no value, you'll feel negatively toward yourself and create unhealthy self-esteem. If you understand you have value and worth, you'll feel positively toward yourself and build healthy self-esteem.

Jackson and Austin were identical twins. At an early age, both boys showed a love of music. In grade school, they both played violin and piano, and were both encouraged by their parents. Both boys also had quiet personalities. They felt more comfortable at home or with one friend than with bigger groups of kids.

Jackson took pride in his musical abilities. He loved performing in the school orchestra and in private recitals. He told himself he was lucky to have this gift. Jackson knew he was shyer than most kids, but he was okay with that. He made a couple of close friends in his music classes and camps and was content to spend time with them playing or composing music. Jackson felt good about himself and was happy with who he was.

Austin had the same level of musical talent as Jackson but didn't feel good about it. He told himself he should have been talented at math like his dad and grandfather, who were successful accountants. He told himself there was something wrong with him because he didn't have this skill. He also told himself he should be more outgoing. He felt embarrassed by his quiet nature and told himself he'd never fit in with other kids. This thought kept him from developing the friendships he did have, so his friends drifted away. Austin felt like he was worthless and believed there was something inherently wrong with him.

It's hard to have healthy self-esteem if we falsely believe there's something wrong with us at our very core. If we believe deep down we're "not as good as everyone else," we're sending ourselves a negative message that ruins our chance for healthy self-esteem.

The truth is, every human being who has ever lived came into this world with value and worth. There has never been an exception. Including you.

Thoughts That Prevent Us from Embracing This Truth

There are many reasons teens might not believe in their own true value; here are some of the common ones:

- They think "different" is wrong.

- They think making mistakes is "bad."

- They judge some people as "better" than others.

- They believe there is a "right" way to look.

When we examine the reality behind these thoughts, we find they don't align with the laws and design of the natural world.

Differences

The natural state of the universe is diversity. Thousands of species of trees, insects, birds, flowers, fish, and mammals confirm this. Diversity—a condition where not everything is the same—keeps our universe alive. Each creature and plant, from mosquitos to redwoods, contributes to the food chain and the environment in a specific way. The diversity of seasons allows the cycle of growth; the ebb and flow of tides sustains the ocean's ecosystem; day and night provide balance between activity and rest. Without diversity, life on our planet couldn't survive.

Learn

Diversity among humans is just as important. It goes without saying we wouldn't last very long if there were only one gender. And what if we all had the same talents or skills? If everyone could only fix cars, who would teach reading? If we were all good at heart transplants, who would harvest our food?

It's our natural state to be different from each other. Our differences form a complex, amazing universe.

It's not uncommon for teens to think there's one "right" way to be. This thought can fuel the feeling we don't measure up and the desire to be like everybody else. However, this thought is a myth, not a truth, and it drives us to reject our authentic self, creating unhealthy self-esteem.

We're not all supposed to be the same—all doing well in chemistry or bowling, all on student council or in band, all writing for the school newspaper or volunteering with kids.

When we understand that every human being has intrinsic value and worth, we recognize the value of diversity. We celebrate our uniqueness and stop trying to be someone else. We know that our differences are gifts that help us reach our full potential and play our distinct part in the universe. We feel good about our authentic self and create healthy self-esteem.

Tanya's family belongs to a faith tradition that doesn't celebrate customary national holidays. This doesn't bother Tanya because she's comfortable with her beliefs and doesn't think there's something wrong with her because she's different from her classmates. She enjoys days off from school for other holidays, but she keeps her own faith's holy days as well. Tanya's self-esteem isn't affected negatively just because her beliefs are different from her friends' beliefs.

Owen is an only child whose father is very successful and generates a high income. His mother doesn't work outside the home; they have a cook, a housekeeper, and a chauffeur, and their house is three times bigger than most kids' houses he knows. Owen feels embarrassed by his family's wealth and tells himself no one will like him because he's different. His self-esteem is affected negatively because of the way he thinks.

Meili loves to play golf. The first time she played miniature golf as a child she won three games in a row. Her parents supported her interest and gave her golf lessons in grade school. Now she's one of two girls on her high school team and loves competing. None of Meili's girlfriends understand her passion. They play basketball and run track and think golf is boring. But they know Meili loves it, and her uniqueness makes her interesting. Meili is happy golfing, and she doesn't care that she's not like her friends. She tells herself it's fun being different, and she creates healthy self-esteem.

Difference is of the essence of humanity.

—John Hume

Explore

Explore how diversity affects your own life by completing these exercises on separate paper or in your journal.

- Name anyone who's influenced how you view diversity. Explain how their beliefs or actions shaped your beliefs. Tell why you'd like to keep or change these beliefs.

- List your three favorite movies, foods, and ways to spend the weekend. Describe what it would be like if there were no differences among the movies, foods, or activities on your list.

- List the reasons you value your best friend. Then list all the ways you're different from each other. Explain how your differences add to your relationship in a positive way.

- Name a group you're in; for example, a study group, sports team, family, or friend group. Identify the different qualities each member brings to the whole. Tell how the group and you, personally, benefit from these differences.

Become

These exercises will help you celebrate your differences. Complete them on separate paper or in your journal.

- Identify the characteristics that make you unique. These could be anything from caring about kids with disabilities to making people laugh when they're sad to excelling at quantum physics. Tell why each of your differences is valuable and how they contribute to the good of the planet.

- Explain how you might use each of your differences to follow a positive path in life. For example, if you care about kids with disabilities, as an adult you might adopt a child with a disability, volunteer in a hospital, or develop new techniques or products to improve their lives.

- List any differences you've found it hard to value in yourself and explain why. Understanding that diversity is valuable, make a list of new thoughts to help you view these differences in a positive light.

Affirm

My differences contribute to the perfection of the universe.

Mistakes

Most of us try to avoid mistakes. We want to get things right the first time so that we don't have to start over, make corrections, or lose an outcome we wanted. When we make mistakes, we might feel frustrated and think negative thoughts like *I really messed up; I'm just not good enough;* or *I'll never get it right.*

Learn

If we see mistakes as something that shouldn't happen, we think *This is bad* when they do. Or we tell ourselves we're "bad"—judging our self-worth by the mistake. We might think we could only accept ourselves if we stopped making mistakes.

In reality, our self-worth has nothing to do with how many mistakes we make. And no one can ever stop making them; no human being ever has. Great leaders, scientists, healers, and parents all make mistakes. They're part of our mortal existence, and they're here to stay.

Think about a keyboard. Does yours have a delete key? When keyboards are manufactured, there aren't two types: those with delete keys for people who make mistakes and those without for people who don't make mistakes. That's because the second group doesn't exist. We all need delete keys.

It's not mistakes themselves that affect self-esteem—it's what we think about them. If we forget that our intrinsic value and worth isn't based on what we do, or if we tell ourselves making mistakes means we're "bad" or "a failure," these negative thoughts create negative feelings. We feel disappointed in ourselves, discouraged about our skills, or angry that we "can never do anything right," and our self-esteem suffers.

Judging mistakes as bad, or as proof of our incompetence, sets us up for a lifetime of disappointment, because no one can achieve the goal of making no more mistakes. But if we see mistakes as a normal part of life, they don't affect our self-worth. If we see them as opportunities to learn, and then act on that, we grow. Then we feel good about ourselves and build healthy self-esteem.

When Kayla struck out three times two games in a row, she felt so embarrassed and angry that she skipped practice the next day and thought about quitting. She told herself she was no good at softball and shouldn't be on the team. She hated the thought of facing her teammates the next week at school. The thoughts she chose about her mistakes contributed to unhealthy self-esteem.

When Matt struck out three times two games in a row, he felt embarrassed and angry. At the next practice, he asked the coach what he could do to improve. The coach gave him some pointers and suggested he practice them before the next game. Matt practiced hard. He told himself he could become a better player. He struck out only once the next week and felt great about his improvement. The thoughts he chose about his mistakes contributed to healthy self-esteem.

When we don't try something because we're afraid to make mistakes, we miss out on the fun, richness, and rewards of life, as well as the chance to build healthy self-esteem. We might even miss a chance to contribute something wonderful to the world.

In the 1970s, 3M chemist Spencer Silver set out to develop a new kind of adhesive. But Silver put in too much of a certain chemical, and his adhesive turned out super-weak instead of super-strong. No one wanted it. A few years later, however, Silver's "mistake" became the adhesive backing for Post-it notes—one of the most popular office products of all time.

In 1905, eleven-year-old Frank Epperson mixed together some powdered soda and water to make himself a fruit drink, a common recipe in those days. He left the mixture outside over the cold night by mistake, and in the morning his stirring stick was stuck in the frozen drink. When he pulled on it, the frozen drink came out in one piece with the stick, and he began to lick it. Some years later, as an adult, Frank introduced the rest of the world to his mistake: the Popsicle.

In 1958, medical researcher Wilson Greatbatch made a mistake and inserted the wrong size resistor into a heartbeat-recording device. He then watched as the circuit pulsed like a human heart. His mistake helped him create the first implantable pacemaker.

Remember, every human being is imperfect, including you. You'll continue to make mistakes for the rest of your life. This has nothing to do with your self-worth.

The only real mistake is the one from which we learn nothing.

—John Powell

Explore

Increase your awareness about the normality of mistakes by completing these exercises on separate paper or in your journal.

- Try to find someone who's never made a mistake, or someone who's decided to stop making mistakes and succeeded. Ask people you know, or search the Internet or other sources.

- Name someone you admire. Describe any mistakes you know he or she has made. If you don't know of any, ask the person.

- Observe people around you for a full day. Record all the mistakes you see being made. These could include someone pulling out too quickly into traffic, a teacher erasing something he has written on the board, or your sister spilling her drink.

- Record your self-messages when you make a mistake. Are they encouraging or discouraging? Do they contribute to healthy self-esteem?

Become

Since no one can stop making mistakes, what's more important is how we respond to them. Complete these exercises on separate paper or in your journal.

- Describe a mistake you made recently that brought up negative feelings about your self-worth. Write new thoughts to change this perspective, and tell how you could use this mistake to learn and grow.

- Write affirmations about accepting mistakes; for example, "Mistakes are a natural part of life," "This is just an example of human error," "I can do my best to fix this and move on." Practice using these statements in your daily life.

- Berating ourselves doesn't fix mistakes or keep us from making more of them; it just creates unhealthy self-esteem. Practice substituting words of forgiveness for self-abuse in your self-messages. Tell what this feels like and how it affects you.

- Pretend you're talking to a younger child who's feeling bad after making a mistake. Describe what you'd say to that child and how you'd explain that mistakes don't change a person's self-worth.

Affirm

My goal is not to stop making mistakes, but to use them to learn and grow.

Judging

The idea that some people are "better" than others runs contrary to the belief that everyone has intrinsic value and worth. We all arrive here as equals, and there's no child, teen, or adult who has more value than another. It also runs contrary to the understanding that we each have a unique purpose on the planet. We'll talk more about that in the next chapter, which is about your authentic self.

Learn

When we think one person is better than another, we're making a judgment, not stating a fact. These are statements of fact:

- I'm taller than my sister.

- These eggs are scrambled.

- Lindsey, Peyton, and Avery are cheerleaders.

- My dog is a terrier, and yours is a Lab.

These are statements of judgment:

- It's cool that I'm taller than my sister.

- Scrambled eggs taste awful.

- Lindsey, Peyton, and Avery are the best cheerleaders in our school.

- Terriers are better than Labs.

Facts are statements we know beyond a doubt to be true. Judgments are statements that can be disputed or questioned. For example, a yardstick will show the fact of our height when we accurately measure our own and our sister's. But the statement "It's cool that I'm taller than my sister" is just a perspective. Other people might argue that they don't like being taller. Watching eggs being tossed and turned as they cook in a pan confirms the fact they are scrambled. But "Scrambled eggs taste awful" is just an opinion. Someone else could disagree, claiming "Scrambled eggs taste wonderful."

We all speak undisputable statements of fact each day. We say, "The temperature is colder today than yesterday," "History class lasted for an hour," or "We ran a 5K last weekend." We also make judgments that could be questioned: "Cold days are great," "History is boring," or "I'm the slowest runner ever."

It's especially common for teens to make judgments. At this time in life we're thinking a lot about what we do or don't like about ourselves. We're deciding who we want to be and seeing how we "measure up." So we often judge the way we think, look, and act and the way other people think, look, and act: "She's too liberal," "He's so scrawny," "She's more fun than me," "I'm nicer than him."

When we judge other people as "better" than us, or when we judge ourselves as "better" than them, we're negatively affecting our self-esteem because we're either feeling good or bad about ourselves based on disputable information, not fact. A judgment is an opinion by someone who needs to judge; it is not a statement of truth. If our self-worth is affected by human judgment, then we believe our value depends on other people's opinions of us.

If we believe some people are "better" than others, we'll always be comparing ourselves to other people for proof of our value. When we find someone we judge "better" than us, we'll feel bad about ourselves. When we find someone we judge ourselves "better" than, we'll feel good. We're putting our self-esteem in the hands of an arbitrary perspective.

It's also important to remember our intrinsic value comes from who we are, not what we do. We may have talents or skills and excel in certain areas—which is a function of diversity. We may be skilled at working with animals or numbers, people or technology. But our skills don't change our intrinsic worth. Winning a dance contest might mean we're the best dancer, but it doesn't give us more value than the other contestants. Dancing is something we do, not who we are.

Judging damages our self-esteem when we act in these ways:

- We forget the intrinsic value and worth of every human being, including ourselves.

- We believe judgments instead of facts.

- We feel good about ourselves by judging ourselves "better" than others.

- We feel bad about ourselves by judging others "better" than us.

- We think someone is a "better" person because of a skill he or she possesses.

David worked as a lifeguard during the summer. He always felt bad about himself because he wasn't as muscular as the other lifeguards. He commented to his friend Anna he felt like a wimp compared to them. "That's a judgment, not a fact," said Anna. "You saved a little boy's life last summer when he fell in the deep end and hit his head on the ladder. That's not wimpy! You're brave and caring, and you do an excellent job. And you're a good friend! Stop judging your self-worth by the size of your arms. The other guards are good, too, but not better. You're a great human being just because you're you."

Nathan had his first assignment for the school newspaper. He was supposed to interview Cody, a senior who had the lead in the play. Nathan felt nervous. He'd never interviewed anyone before, and Cody was very popular and a great actor. Nathan hoped he didn't sound stupid or stutter when he asked questions. When Cody asked Nathan what other articles he'd written, Nathan was too embarrassed to admit this was his first, so he lied and said he couldn't remember. That sounded weird and made him feel worse! Then Nathan noticed Cody was perspiring and his hands were shaking. Cody said, "I'm sorry, I didn't mean to pry. I'm just nervous about what you'll write about me—I've never been interviewed before. Writers are so smart, and you could make me sound really stupid." "Seriously?" said Nathan. "And I'm nervous because you're a senior and so popular." Both boys started laughing. "Wow," said Cody. "We both judged the other as better, and it made us feel bad about ourselves. Just goes to show we're all the same inside."

It is not for me to judge the life of another.

—Herman Hesse

Explore

Take a look at judging in your own life by answering these questions. Use separate paper or write in your journal.

- Who do you compare yourself to when you want to feel better about yourself? Does your judgment actually make you better or more valuable than that other person?

- Who do you compare yourself to and then feel bad about yourself in comparison? Does your judgment actually make that person better or more valuable than you?

- Listen to conversations between your friends and yourself. Observe how often any of you makes judgments and how you feel when doing this. Tell what purpose judgments serve for your friend group.

- Record your self-messages today. Tell what feeling each message creates for you. Explain whether each message is based on judgment or fact.

- Describe how judging affects your self-esteem.

Become

Work on releasing judgment by completing these exercises. Use separate paper or write in your journal.

- Record your thoughts of comparison and the judgments that follow. For example, your comparison *Asha's hair is darker than mine* might be followed by the judgment *She's so much prettier than me.* Then try changing each judgment to acceptance. For example, *She's so much prettier than me* could be *It's okay that we're different.*

- Describe one day of your life with fact, not opinion. For example, say, "I babysat my little brother," (fact) but not "I babysat my annoying little brother" (opinion). Tell how it feels to try to stop judging.

- Record your thoughts of self-judgment. Tell how they affect your self-esteem.

- Notice when you judge yourself for something you do, either positively or negatively. Remind yourself that while choosing positive actions creates healthy self-esteem, it doesn't change your intrinsic self-worth.

Affirm

My value doesn't change when I compare myself to others.

Looks

Our intrinsic value has nothing to do with our looks. The size, shape, color, or texture of our bodies are physical properties that don't add or subtract anything from our worth. Babies born with no hair are just as valuable as those with a head of curls. Skin color, shape of eyes, or size of biceps doesn't affect the value of the person inside the container.

Learn

We can get mixed up about looks. We're born with no opinion of our bodies, but as we grow we get messages about "right" and "wrong" ways to look. Some of them sound like these:

- "Your hair is too curly; you need a straightener."

- "Your hair is too straight; you need a curling iron."

- "You're so pale; go outside and get some color."

- "You don't want freckles; better stay out of the sun."

- "You're putting on weight; watch what you eat."

- "No one will date a skeleton; better put on a few pounds."

The idea that looks are very important is maintained by a multibillion-dollar beauty industry. This industry promotes the myth that the "right" look will make us "right" and bring happiness, love, and problem-free lives. So we spend money on products and services that promise to bring this. The system works well because the beauty ideal is actually impossible to achieve. Photos of the "best" look are computer-altered and airbrushed, so even supermodels aren't actually good enough to sell what they're promoting. A "right" look is also contrary to the truth about differences. Clearly all humans are not supposed to look alike. This gap between what's ideal and what's real keeps us spending money trying to achieve the impossible.

Most of us want to feel good about our looks. We take care of our hair, skin, and clothes, and we check the mirror once in a while. We like our looks on some days and not on others, but this doesn't make or break our self-worth. Our self-esteem stays healthy even with a bad haircut, an acne breakout, or a sweater that doesn't fit right. We know the source of our value runs deeper than what we see on the surface. We also know that these conditions are temporary and that there are other things to think about—the movie date Friday, the test Monday, or the yearbook meeting next week. Our daily looks don't change the way we value ourselves.

There's nothing wrong with paying attention to grooming and fashion. But if we connect our self-worth with the appearance of our container, we damage our self-esteem. Some of us put too much importance on appearance. When we think we don't look good, it interferes in our lives. If our bangs won't lie flat, we skip class to fix them. If we can't find something to wear that we feel good in, we cancel our plans. If our pants feel too tight, we put our health at risk by going on fad diets.

This also works in reverse. If we think we're better than someone else because we look more like an advertisement, that's not healthy self-esteem. If one of our life goals is to look like the beauty ideal in order to be happy, that's not healthy self-esteem either.

Any time we let our looks control our self-esteem, we're giving away our power. We've let a made-up ideal control our worth. We've let strangers who know nothing about us decide whether we like ourselves or not. Equating our self-worth with the way we look denies our intrinsic human value and is not a characteristic of healthy self-esteem.

Dylan had always been the shortest in his class. He had a small frame, and his doctor predicted he wouldn't grow taller than five foot two, which was short for a male. In grade school, kids made fun of him and called him Squirt and Half-Pint. Dylan learned to ignore them and focus on what he liked about himself. He had a crazy sense of humor, was a great downhill skier, and had two awesome best friends. Dylan didn't base his worth on the way he looked, and his self-esteem was healthy. He knew the size of his body didn't have anything to do with his value as a human being. Dylan became an esteemed leader in his community.

Skylar was smart, talented, and fun to be around. She had plenty of friends, was respected by her teachers, and was appreciated at the animal shelter where she volunteered. But Skylar didn't think as much of herself as everyone else did. She weighed herself every morning and was never happy with the number on the scale. She thought she'd feel good about herself only by losing weight. She skipped parties if she was feeling "fat" and severely restricted her food intake. Sometimes she wouldn't eat breakfast or lunch and would feel dizzy in gym class. Skylar's family and friends loved her, but her self-esteem was tied to her looks, and when she didn't like what she saw in the mirror she didn't like herself.

When you start looking at people's hearts instead of their face, life becomes clear.

—Author unknown

Explore

Explore how the beauty industry affects your self-esteem by completing the following activities. Use separate paper or write in your journal.

- Record the ads you see on television, radio, the Internet, on billboards, or in print that promote a "right" way to look. Tell how they affect you.

- List any products or services you see or hear about in your house, in stores, or elsewhere that are designed to help people look "better." See how long it takes you to get one hundred items. Describe your reaction to this activity.

- From what you see in advertising and media, describe the ideal look that's sold to you by the beauty industry.

- Tell how you feel about yourself when you're happy with your looks and when you're not. If your feelings change, does your intrinsic value actually change? Are you a more valuable person when you're happy with your looks and less valuable when you're not?

Become

Claim your intention to take back control of your feelings about your looks from a big business. Complete the following exercises on separate paper or in your journal.

- Find ads that promote a beauty ideal that's unachievable by the average person. Reinforce your refusal to let a business tell you how to feel about your body by shredding or (safely) destroying these ads in some way. Explain how letting strangers tell you how to feel about your body has affected you. Tell how it feels to take charge of your feelings about your body.

- Write the names of the three most important people in your life. Tell what makes each of them valuable to you. Then ask one of these people what makes you valuable to him or her. Do looks create anyone's value?

- Make a list of twenty-five or more ways your body has helped you since you were born, no matter what it looked like. This could be anything from being able to see colors, wake up in the morning, heal a cut, recover from a cold, or win a Frisbee tournament.

- Describe what you as an individual with your own unique talents and strengths would like to contribute to the planet during your lifetime. (Making a positive change in society? Love or caring for others? Discovering a cure for disease? Helping people less fortunate? Having good looks?)

Affirm

People's looks do not affect their value and worth.

Three Friends

In a faraway land lived a peacock, an eagle, and a humming-bird. Each creature was happy and content with itself and its life until one day when the three met. The birds had never seen one another before, and they were awestruck.

"You're so very beautiful!" said the eagle to the peacock. "Look at your brilliant colors, your markings, your exquisite feathers!" The eagle looked at his own drab brown coloring and plain feathers in dismay. *I would be so much happier if I were a peacock*, the eagle thought.

At the same time, the hummingbird was admiring the eagle. "Look at your wingspan, your size, your strength!" the little hummingbird said. "If only I were bigger and as powerful and majestic as you, I would have a much better life!"

The peacock, meanwhile, was observing the hummingbird as she flitted quickly and adeptly around the eagle. "Oh, look at the agility and grace of this tiny hummingbird as she dances in the air! If only I could move like that!" the peacock said. "My days would be filled with so much more joy if I had the body of a hummingbird."

The three creatures went back to their homes and spent every day trying to become the bird they had admired. The hummingbird affixed large feathers to her tiny form so she could be powerful like the eagle, but the feathers were so big and heavy that she couldn't walk, much less soar. The peacock tried cutting off his long tail feathers so he could dance in the air like the hummingbird, but he became unbalanced and couldn't move without tipping over. The eagle lamented his dull, plain body every time he saw his reflection in a lake, but he couldn't change his coloring, so he became sullen and depressed. The three birds' happiness and contentment vanished. Instead of living out their years celebrating the beautiful creatures they had always been, they spent all their energy trying to reach an impossible goal and felt only sorrow and disappointment.

My Greatest Value, Potential, and Power Lie in My Authentic Self

When we're discovering who we want to be, it's normal to look at others as role models. We admire traits of a friend, parent, celebrity, or fictional character. We might even try adopting some of their opinions or behaviors. It's healthy to educate ourselves about other people's lives and choices and how they achieved their goals. But ultimately, the only person we'll have success being is ourselves. We're all created in a unique, individual pattern different from everyone else's. So even if we spend every minute of every day trying to be someone else, we can never attain that goal.

Sometimes we try to be someone else because we hold beliefs like these:

- *Being someone else will make me happier.*

- *Being someone else will make me more successful.*

- *Being someone else will make other people like me more.*

- *Being someone else will make me like myself more.*

However, these beliefs aren't true. Even if we became very much like someone else, we'd quickly realize that the energy this never-ending task requires is enormous and we can never actually achieve this impossible goal. Then our thoughts would sound more like these:

- *Trying to be someone else is draining me.*

- *Trying to be someone else is creating failure, not success, because I can't achieve this.*

- *Trying to be someone else doesn't make other people like me more, because they don't know the real me.*

- *Trying to be someone else doesn't make me like myself more, because I'm rejecting who I really am.*

Who Is Your Authentic Self?

Your authentic self is who you are at the very core of your being. It's the unique, individual combination of cells and energy patterns that compose your body, mind, and spirit.

Your greatest value, potential, and power lie in your authentic self because it's who you're supposed to be. Look at the natural world. What if a sea turtle spent its whole life trying to be a dolphin? Or a towering oak a delicate rose? They would fail, of course, and miss out on becoming the amazing creatures they are and filling the purpose only they can fill.

Sometimes people do the same thing. We spend our lives trying—and failing—to be someone else and miss the success and happiness we'd attain by developing our authentic self.

Following your authentic self is the key to creating the life you want. The better you know, trust, and express your authentic self, the more valuable you are, the more of your unique potential you can reach, and the more power you have to create healthy self-esteem.

Jada watched her favorite reality show every week to see what her idol, Marianna, was doing. She paid close attention to how Marianna acted, her clothes, her hair, and even the phrases she used in conversation. Jada believed if she were more like Marianna, she'd be more popular and happier with herself. The problem was when Jada tried dressing, acting, and talking like Marianna, she came across as fake and confusing. Her friends wondered who she really was, and people didn't know how to relate to her—she seemed so different from anyone their age. The more Jada tried to copy Marianna, the more people turned away from her. They just didn't feel they could connect with her.

When Denzel was younger, he looked up to his older brother, Dewayne. Dewayne was a starter on the basketball team, made people laugh, and took honors science classes. Denzel thought that if he did everything like Dewayne he'd have a great life. So he tried out for the basketball team, but didn't make it; tried memorizing jokes, but always forgot the punch line; tried an honors physics class, but barely passed. "What are you trying to do, be your brother?" his mom asked. Denzel admitted, "Well, yes." "Don't you know you'll only be successful being your-self?" she said. "You're a great pitcher—why don't you go out for baseball? Take honors English—you're a good writer! And stop telling those bad jokes! Your friends like you when you're yourself, not a Dewayne wannabe."

It's important to remember your healthy authentic self is in line with your positive gifts and leads to your highest potential.

If you think you're being true to your authentic self but are getting into trouble, talk to an adult you trust about how to stop and rethink your choices.

Reasons We Reject Our Authentic Self

We may turn away from our authentic self if we think it isn't good enough. Or, we may not realize we're rejecting our authentic self because we've never known to pay attention.

These are some common reasons we reject our authentic self:

- expectations placed on us
- roles we play
- believing there is "greener grass"
- not accepting that we're on a journey

When we understand how these factors influence us, we can make conscious choices to respect our authentic self and create healthy self-esteem.

Expectations

An expectation is the belief something will be a certain way. For example, we may have the daily expectations that the sun will rise, we will eat lunch, the school will be open when we get there, and we will have fun at our friend's party. Throughout our life, we may have expectations that we will get passing grades, finish high school, live with our parents until we're old enough to move out, and get a job and support ourselves someday.

If the expectations are strong and we aren't sure enough of who we are, we might turn away from our authentic self to fulfill them. Expectations can also give us direction, and following them can feel easier than discovering the path of our authentic self.

Learn

Many expectations in our lives come from other people, such as our parents:

- We expect you to keep your room clean.

- We expect you to come home on time.

- We expect you to pass your classes.

- We expect you to do your chores without us nagging you.

Or our friends:

- I expect you to keep my secret.

- I expect you to be honest with me.

- I expect you to show up when you say you will.

- I expect you to lend me lunch money when I'm short.

Or the society we live in:

- You're expected to get an education.

- You're expected not to shoplift.

- You're expected to be loyal to your country.

- You're expected to obey traffic laws.

Expectations from family, friends, and society can be in line with your authentic self or not. Your parents might expect you to follow their political views but you don't agree with them. Fulfilling their expectation rejects your authentic self. Your friend group might expect you to help them cheat on a test but you don't believe in cheating. Fulfilling their expectation rejects your authentic self.

Your best friend might expect you to lie to her boyfriend about where she is, but you don't believe in disrespecting people like that. If you explain why you won't fulfill her expectation and follow through, you're acting in line with your authentic self. Society might expect you to choose a career that's typical for your gender, but you might be talented in an area that's more typical of the opposite gender. If you follow your natural talent you won't meet society's expectations, but you'll be true to your authentic self.

If we let others' expectations pull us too far from our authentic self, we usually feel discomfort. We get a deep sense that we're not acting the way that's right for us. This eats away at healthy self-esteem. The opposite is also true: when we stay true to our authentic self despite others' expectations, we feel at peace with ourselves. This creates healthy self-esteem.

Savannah always wanted to be a teacher. She loved helping kids learn and grow and creating ways to make learning fun. She took child development classes and volunteered at a day care center. While Savannah's parents wouldn't keep her from her dream, she knew it wasn't their first choice. Her father warned her teaching wasn't a high-paying career, it could be hard to find a job, and she'd be working lots of extra hours. He said he'd expected her to use her creativity to go into advertising or public relations. When Savannah got into a competitive college, most of her classmates were going into business, medicine, or law. They asked her why she didn't want to do something "bigger" than teach kids. Savannah changed her major to business. After she graduated, she tried several jobs in advertising but always quit. Finally she went back to school for her teaching certificate and fulfilled her dream. Savannah had thought she'd feel better by following other people's expectations, but when she rejected her authentic self she was never really happy.

Ethan was the quarterback of the football team. He was smart, handsome, and good at almost anything he tried. He played piano by ear, wrote computer programs practically in his sleep, and was taking flying lessons. His teammates were rowdy guys who liked to party and hang out on weekends. They group dated and their girlfriends all got along, too. For a while, Ethan felt expected to party with his teammates. But while he got along with them, he just didn't enjoy their lifestyle. He went to a few parties at the beginning of the year, but later he opted out. Ethan knew he could fake having fun, but he was much happier watching movies or writing code with his two close friends, Jason and Cole. His classmates were surprised Ethan didn't run with the more popular crowd, but he didn't mind. He didn't want to waste his time being someone he wasn't. He felt happiest, had the healthiest self-esteem, and knew his greatest value, potential, and power lay in being his authentic self.

It's not your responsibility to want the life that others want for you.

—Colin Wright

Explore

The following exercises will help you discover expectations that affect your life. Complete them on separate paper or in your journal.

- Make a list of expectations you feel from your family. Put an "A" for "authentic" next to those that are in line with your authentic self, and an "E" for "expectation" next to those that are not. Write about what you observe.

- Identify two or more expectations put on you by your friends. Explain whether or not you fulfill these expectations and how this feels to you.

- Describe any social expectations you feel, and give examples of how you do or do not fulfill these in your daily life.

- Explain how your self-esteem is affected when you fulfill expectations that are in line with your authentic self and when you fulfill expectations that are not.

Become

Identify the characteristics of your authentic self before you're influenced by expectations. Complete these exercises on separate paper or write in your journal.

- Sit quietly and comfortably, close your eyes, and take a gentle breath. Open your heart and mind. Ask yourself: *Who do I want to be in the universe?* Let the answers come without rushing them. Think about the kind of person you want to be before you're affected by expectations. How would you like others to describe you; what would you like to be known for? Record your thoughts.

- If you had no limitations—mental, financial, physical, or spiritual—what would you love to do with your life? Describe what your dream would look like if you could make anything you wanted come true for yourself in your lifetime.

- Make a list of beliefs you learned from your parents or other adults. These might include thoughts such as *Everyone should go to college; Manners are important; You should respect your elders; Life is an adventure; God loves you;* or *Giving is better than receiving.* Explain which beliefs you agree with and which you don't. If you don't agree with a belief, explain why and rewrite it to be more in line with what you believe.

- Without being concerned about other people's reactions, explain your personal beliefs about two or more of the following topics.

  preserving the environment

  casual sex

  the existence of a higher power

  drugs and alcohol

  the best voting age

the death penalty

school dress codes

abortion

divorce

life after death

bullying

civil rights

animal rights

freedom

Affirm

I don't let expectations lead me away from my authentic self.

Roles

A role is a part we play in a certain situation or with a certain group of people, almost like the part an actor takes in a play. We all play roles in our family, our friend groups, and society.

Learn

In a family, birth order, parents' expectations, and each member's personality affect which role kids take. In a friend group, personality traits, communication skills, and interpersonal comfort levels can affect who plays which roles. In a society, all these factors and more combine to determine the roles we play as we mature. Our roles develop over time and affect the way we relate to other people.

These are a few common roles:

- clown—someone who's often making people laugh

- caretaker—someone who is concerned about the other group members and tries to help them with their problems

- rebel—someone who rejects authority, breaks rules, or gets into trouble

- scapegoat—someone who gets blamed when something goes wrong, whether it's their fault or not

- peacemaker—someone who makes sure everyone gets along with each other and tries to work out conflicts between group members

Sometimes our roles are in line with who we really are. Other times, our roles can get in the way of developing our authentic self. As with expectations, when we're not completely sure of our authentic self, we might play roles simply because they're familiar and provide us with "guidelines" for how to think, feel, and act. People might continue to play roles because it's easier than trying to break out of them or discover their authentic self.

When our roles are in line with our authentic self and help us feel good about who we are and how we act, they create healthy self-esteem. Roles that don't reflect our true self, or that make us feel bad about who we are and how we act, do the opposite.

Our ability to move between roles or change roles can also affect how we feel about ourselves. If we feel trapped in a role that isn't in line with our authentic self, we may feel negatively about ourselves. If we believe we have a choice about our roles, or we are positively fulfilled by them, they can create healthy self-esteem.

Continuing to play roles because they're familiar might seem easier at first, but over time we feel the uncomfortable gap between the role we're playing and the person we really are. When we move away from our role and toward our authentic self, we build healthy self-esteem. If we stay in the inauthentic role, we continue feeling stuck and uncomfortable and miss out on the chance to develop our authentic self and our full value, potential, and power. Our self-esteem doesn't get healthier.

Tyler's parents had a marriage filled with conflict, and he often tried to make peace between them. Tyler's mom suffered from anxiety and depression, and she looked to Tyler for emotional support. His dad had a hard time managing anger, and he often exploded verbally at Tyler and then apologized. Tyler was naturally sensitive to other people's needs, and while he was growing up his skills as an "emotional supporter" were strengthened. He became an attentive listener and instinctively knew when to intervene in arguments and when to stay out. He learned how to read people's feelings and which communication styles worked and which didn't. Tyler knew both his parents were good people and loved him, but their own struggles got in the way of their relationships. Tyler took a psychology class and became interested in helping people work out problems. His family role of "counselor" felt in line with his authentic self and led him to a career as a psychologist, where he enjoyed helping families overcome emotional struggles. Tyler's family role was in line with his authentic self. He expanded his value, potential, and power and created healthy self-esteem by staying true to this in a productive way.

Krishana was the youngest of five. Her older sisters loved to baby her, and her older brothers were protective of her. Krishana grew up learning that other people would always cushion her blows and watch out for her. As Krishana got older, she was interested in new activities. She asked to try out for gymnastics, but her family was afraid she'd get injured. She was elected to student council, but her siblings did so much of the campaigning that she felt like she hadn't won the position on her own. Krishana had a curious and brave spirit, and the older she got, the more uncomfortable she felt in the role of "baby" of the family. She was tired of everyone expecting her to be fragile and weak. Krishana didn't feel she was being true to her authentic self when she let her siblings overprotect her. One day she explained how she felt. She wanted a chance to be herself, not just their little sister. Krishana knew her greatest value, potential, and power lay in following her authentic self, not being stuck in a role that no longer fit her. Krishana's healthy self-esteem grew when she moved past her role and developed her authentic self.

It's like you're a character in this book that everyone around you is writing, and suddenly you have to say, "I'm sorry, but this role isn't right for me." And you have to start writing your own life and doing your own thing.

—David Levithan

Explore

These exercises will help identify the roles you play in different groups. Use separate paper or write in your journal.

- Name the people in your immediate and extended family, including yourself. Write down the roles you think each person plays in your family. Feel free to come up with your own.

instigator	peacemaker
clown	observer
critic	judge
baby	scapegoat
bully	boss
counselor	confronter
intellectual	hero
moralist	goody-goody
disciplinarian	free spirit
overachiever	blamer
rebel	tough guy
commander in chief	whiner

- List your friend groups, such as "school," "volleyball," "neighborhood," "job," or others. Next to each, copy the roles you think you play in that group. Feel free to come up with your own. How do your family and friend group roles compare? Tell whether you like playing these roles and why.

partier	critic
daredevil	rebel
voice of reason	brain
peacemaker	planner
romantic	bully
joker	ghost
leader	follower
connector	victim
listener	speaker
counselor	comic

- Describe how society affects your thoughts, feelings, and actions in any of these areas:

religion	physical appearance
education	manners
politics	morality
substance use	work ethic
sexual behavior	charity

- Explain whether these thoughts, feelings, and actions are in line with your authentic self.

- Describe how your roles do or don't build healthy self-esteem.

Become

Thinking about how your roles align with your authentic self is the first step in deciding which of them are or aren't creating healthy self-esteem. Answer these prompts on separate paper or in your journal.

- What do you do or say that keeps you playing your current roles? Explain what you'd have to do or say differently to make your roles more like your authentic self.

- Describe the roles you think would create the healthiest self-esteem for you. Tell what you could change to make this happen.

- Write down the word in each of the pairs below that most appeals to your authentic self.

walk	ride	save	discard
cook	eat out	cold	hot
write	speak	numbers	words
focus	dream	day	night
books	TV	ocean	mountains
home	away	talk	listen

plane	train	rock	rap
hard	soft	school	work
bath	shower	air	ground
fast	slow	jeans	sweats
formal	casual	sugar	salt
city	country	sitcom	movie
comedy	drama	alone	together
cola	clear	spring	fall
sandals	sneakers	play	watch

Do your choices reflect the roles you like to play or those you don't?

- Describe how playing your roles has affected your life in the past, how it affects your life in the present, and how it may affect your life in the future.

Affirm

I can choose which roles I play.

"Greener Grass"

The saying "The grass is always greener on the other side of the fence" comes from the idea of someone looking over a fence and thinking their neighbor's yard is greener, healthier, and more beautiful than their own. This proverb is used when we think someone else's life is better than ours, but it's always understood as a misperception. Standing directly in our own lawn, we can see all its flaws. From a distance, across the fence, the neighbors' lawn appears perfect. But getting closer, we see their weeds, dry spots, bugs, and bare patches, just like ours.

Learn

This "greener grass" idea applies when we view another person and have thoughts like these:

- *Her life is better than mine.*

- *His life is easier than mine.*

- *She has a perfect life.*

- *He doesn't have any problems.*

If we believe these thoughts, we might reject our authentic self. When we imagine another person's life is without flaws, we think we'd rather be that person than ourselves.

The important fact to remember is that no one is perfect or has a perfect life. We see others from a distance. Closer in, with more information, we see the truth: everyone is imperfect, has challenges, and struggles in some way. Each person's challenges may be different from ours, but they still exist.

This idea is similar to the comparing and judging idea in principle 2: thinking some people are "better" than others. Thinking someone is "better" is a judgment of worth—they have more value because of what they do or say or how they look. Thinking someone has "greener grass" means we believe that person's life is problem-free: his face never breaks out, she always has enough money, he's always having fun, she has the perfect family, house, clothes—no weeds in the lawn. Neither of these ideas is true, and believing them does not create healthy self-esteem.

If we believe other people have perfect lives while we don't, we create a negative attitude about ourselves. This damages our self-esteem because we're rejecting who we are. We shut down any chance for our authentic self to live and flourish, and we can't develop our full potential.

Conversely, when we understand all people have some weeds in their lawns somewhere—some challenge, struggle, or something they don't like—even if we can't see it—it reminds us we're all traveling the same road, with joy and beauty, potholes and bumps. Absolutely no one has a perfectly smooth path. This reminds us of our equality to all other humans and builds healthy self-esteem.

As we meet more and more people, we get more glimpses into others' lives, and it becomes clear that no matter one's age, background, or walk of life, no matter how intelligent, talented, or prosperous, there isn't one person without challenges. Those could be personal, professional, mental, emotional, financial, or any other kind of challenge. No one else might see them. But they are there. We all have weeds in our lawns.

Kaylee was doing homework in the bleachers when she saw Max down on the track alone, jumping hurdles. Max was a year older and seemed the perfect boy. He took all honors classes and was a star athlete, handsome, and fun. Kaylee watched as he paced his breath and stretched between each run. He looked so focused and calm, so physically and mentally strong. When Max saw her, he came up to say hi. "You are so amazing," Kaylee blurted out. "What?" Max said. "You're the most confident person I know," Kaylee said. "You're so perfectly in tune with yourself.

You always know the right thing to do and say. I wish I had your grades, your personality, and your life." Max laughed in surprise. "Wow!" he said. "You sure have an unreal picture of me! Did you know I come out here alone because I get too nervous when I practice with the team? I have social anxiety almost all the time. I run and go to counseling to manage it. Thanks for the compliment, Kaylee, but I'm no different from anybody else. You just don't see everything from the outside."

Amanda felt nervous about sharing a room with Maria at the tennis competition. Whenever Amanda saw her, Maria was surrounded by friends, laughing and smiling. She'd been Homecoming Queen and was dating the nicest boy in school. Amanda judged Maria as the perfect girl with the perfect life, not like herself—always struggling with homework, friend problems, or mood swings. When the girls were unpacking, Maria told Amanda she was glad they were roommates. "There's so much pressure when I'm with my other friends," she said. "They hold me up to a standard I just can't meet. Sometimes I want to run away. Last year when my parents got divorced I didn't have anyone to talk to. I almost did run away. Maybe I can relax and be more my real self with you." Amanda was stunned. By the end of the trip, Amanda realized that Maria's life was no more perfect than hers. She just never knew about Maria's struggles because she didn't see them. When she found out, Amanda stopped rejecting her own authentic self, and her self-esteem grew healthier.

If the grass is always greener on the other side, then the other side must think your grass looks greener, too.

—Author unknown

Explore

Complete the following exercises to better understand the "greener grass" perspective. Use separate paper or write in your journal.

- Take a picture of something from fifty feet away, then twenty feet, then ten feet, then one foot. List all the details of this object that you can see in each photo. Explain how this illustrates the "greener grass" idea.

- Describe things you know about people in your family because of your close perspective that outsiders wouldn't know.

- List the people you know who look like they have a "perfect" life, and tell why you think this. Then pretend you can see closer details of their lives. Describe any challenges they might have with family, friends, health, emotions, school, job, self-esteem, or anything else.

Become

These exercises demonstrate how the "greener grass" idea affects your self-esteem. Complete them on separate paper or in your journal.

- Explain how your self-esteem might be affected if you found the diary of the most "perfect" person you know and read about all his or her personal troubles and flaws.

- You're aware of your challenges because you see them up close every day. What if people were looking at your life from "over the fence"? Describe what they might see to make them think you had no problems. How would they describe your "perfect" life without your close-up view?

- How does believing some people don't have any "weeds in their lawn" affect your desire to be your authentic self? How does it affect your self-esteem? What thoughts could you choose to help you better embrace and respect your authentic self and build healthy self-esteem?

Affirm

No human being has a life without challenges.

Accepting Our Journey

We begin our life path as newborn babies—having each entered the world with intrinsic value and worth. Then we move through the years as if we're traveling down a road. Everyone's journey is filled with joy and sorrow, easy and hard times, smooth and rough spots. As we go along, we meet people, have experiences, learn, and grow.

Learn

When we understand the journey, we realize that as long as we're alive there is always farther to go. Knowing there is always more to learn and more steps to take helps us accept that there will never be a time when we "know it all" or have "accomplished it all." As human beings, we are works in progress. We continue to develop the value, potential, and power of our authentic self until we take our last breath.

In our teen years, especially, we're moving forward on our journey. This is an amazing time when our brain development lets us think about ourselves in deeper ways. We're learning to walk the road without our parents right next to us. We're stepping beside our friends more. We're no longer children, but we're not adults yet either. We can see so many paths in front of us, and so many ways to travel them. This is an exciting time and a challenging time. Thinking about our choices can feel fun and stimulating yet also confusing and daunting.

Sometimes we feel annoyed at ourselves for making mistakes, taking too long to learn something, or encountering yet another challenge. We may feel angry for making decisions we regret, or frustrated and impatient because we don't know exactly who we are or why we're changing. We might feel discouraged if we don't think we're growing or achieving our goals fast enough.

When we feel upset about our slow progress or not understanding who we are, we're thinking negatively about ourselves. This turns us away from our authentic self and damages our self-esteem. Understanding life as a journey, not a destination—or an ongoing process, not one point in time—helps us accept confusion and uncertainty. We know our authentic self will evolve over time, in different ways, for as long as we live. There will always be times we change directions, move slower or faster, or turn around and backtrack. This is normal and doesn't mean we've done something wrong or aren't progressing fast enough. It just means we're on the road, moving along like everyone else.

It's important to remember no one ever knows everything—about life or themselves—at any given time. Especially for teens, it's normal to not know! This is the way of adolescence—you won't find yourself by reading one book, talking to one person, or making one decision. Discovering your authentic self is a process; it doesn't happen overnight. Accepting your authentic self as a work in progress creates healthy self-esteem.

"I feel so scared and down," Rahul told his guidance counselor. "I can't decide on next semester's classes." "Why the fear and depression?" asked Mr. Amis. "I'm only a sophomore," Rahul said. "And I'm getting college information with application requirements and questions about majors, and I don't even know what to take next semester! Why don't I know what I want?" "It's okay," Mr. Amis said. "The college questions are just preliminary. You don't have to have the answers now—in fact, you can't. Let's list the classes you need to graduate from high school; that's all you have to know today. Other answers will come step by step. None of us knows who we'll be several years from now, especially teens. There's nothing wrong with not knowing, Rahul. Life is a journey, and we can't always see around the bends, but that's okay! Accept that and you'll feel better about yourself."

Chloe complained to her older sister, Jordan, "I don't know what's wrong with me! Last year Brianna was my best friend, and now she drives me crazy. Yesterday I bought the same shoes I loved last summer, and now I hate the way they look. I was always happy being a tomboy, and now I want to be feminine. Why do I keep changing? I wish I were someone else!" "That's normal," Jordan said. "You're a human being. I went through the same thing and felt frustrated, too. But as time goes on, you discover yourself." Then she laughed. "Of course, you never get all the answers. But that's okay; it's all part of growing. Learn to accept it and you won't feel so down on yourself—you'll start to enjoy the ride." Chloe realized Jordan was right. When she viewed growing and changing as something "wrong," she abandoned her authentic self and damaged her self-esteem. If she accepted her changes as normal, she no longer felt bad about herself.

When you become comfortable with uncertainty, infinite possibilities open up in your life.

—Eckhart Tolle

Explore

Self-understanding and self-knowledge develop over time for as long as you live. Answer the following prompts on separate paper or in your journal.

- Describe what you knew for sure about yourself when you were four, eight, and ten years old. How did your self-knowledge change over time?

- Ask someone older than you—a parent, grandparent, friend, teacher, or other adult—to tell you what they still don't know about themselves or life, despite having been on the planet a lot longer than you.

- Make a list of unanswered questions you have about yourself or your life. Rate them in order of how important they are to you. Which ones are the hardest to not know the answers to, and which are the easiest?

- Describe yourself today—what you value, what you enjoy, your inner qualities. Tell how many of these characteristics were known to you five years ago.

Become

Get to know the person you are today and help yourself accept uncertainty by completing these exercises. Use separate paper or write in your journal.

- Complete the following sentences:

  If I won the lottery, I would…

  If I could live anywhere, it would be…

  If I could have three wishes, they would be…

  Describe how your answers might be different in ten years.

- List five words to describe your authentic self as you know it today. Explain how these words might change over time.

- Describe your ideal life five years from now and then ten years from now. Think about how you'd like to spend your time, the relationships you'd like, and how and where you'd like to live. Explain why these ideals may or may not change over time.

- How is your self-esteem affected when you tell yourself you should know all the answers to your questions? How is it affected when you tell yourself it's okay not to know?

- Describe anything you know about your authentic self today. When you're done, write yourself a reminder that for today, this is just enough to know.

Affirm

My greatest value, potential, and power lie in my authentic self. My understanding of who that is will continue to evolve over time.

part 2

power-filled choices

We've talked about the power you have by choosing your beliefs. You've learned that you create healthy self-esteem when you hold these beliefs:

- My self-esteem is in my hands.

- Every human being has intrinsic value and worth, including me.

- My greatest value, potential, and power lie in my authentic self.

You also give yourself a strong mental base for choosing behaviors that sustain that self-esteem.

You bring your beliefs to every life situation, every relationship, and every challenge. When you believe in your equality to others, in the value of your unique self, and that the state of your self-esteem is your own choice, you have the confidence to choose behaviors that are in line with those beliefs.

Just as you control what you choose to think and believe, you also control how you choose to act in every situation.

Gabrielle felt discouraged. She couldn't keep up in her classes, her best friend had left her for other kids, and she was tired of her parents nagging her. She decided her life was awful and sat in front of the TV every night eating ice cream. She told herself there was nothing she could do so she wasn't going to try. Because of the choices she made, Gabrielle's situation didn't improve. In fact, it got worse.

John felt discouraged. Things kept going wrong—with his grades, his friends, and his family. But he told his uncle, "I refuse to give up! I'm going to push through this and turn things around. I'm going to catch up on my sleep, get organized, and talk things out with my friends and family." Because of the choices he made, John's situation changed. In fact, it got better.

The three principles presented in this section encompass twelve specific power-filled choices you can make about how to act. They explain how choosing positive actions will create healthy self-esteem.

The Wolf

One evening a wise elder told her grandchildren a story about life. She said to them,

"A fight is going on inside you. It is a fight between two wolves. One wolf represents fear, anger, envy, sorrow, regret, greed, arrogance, self-pity, guilt, resentment, inferiority, lies, false pride, superiority, and ego. The other stands for joy, peace, love, hope, sharing, serenity, humility, kindness, benevolence, friendship, empathy, generosity, truth, compassion, and faith. The same fight going on inside you is inside every other person, too."

One grandchild thought for a minute and then asked, "Grandmother, which wolf wins?"

The wise elder replied, "The one you feed."

Feeding the Positive Grows the Positive

To increase anything in your life, give it energy. Concentrate on it. The more focus and energy you give it, the more it will expand. Feed something with your attention and it will grow. Starve it by leaving it alone and it will diminish.

When we go through life focusing on what we don't like, what we don't want, or what we wish were different, all our energy goes toward negativity. Whatever fills our mind creates our feelings and our experiences. When we feed our minds negativity, that's what we experience and create more of, and that's how we feel about ourselves.

The following section explains four power-filled choices that are based on the principle "Feeding the positive grows the positive." They describe thoughts and actions that feed and build the positive in our lives. Making these positive choices increases our successes, happiness, and positive feelings about ourselves, creating healthy self-esteem.

The Power of Attitude

There are many things we can't control in life. Friends move away, parents divorce, people die. We don't get the teacher we want or the job we want, we don't win the election or make the team. Disappointments and challenges lie around every bend.

However, there's something we bring to every situation that controls whether our experience is positive or negative. That is our attitude.

Learn

Attitude is like a lens through which we see everything in life. It's like putting on a pair of glasses: If we wear glasses with orange lenses, everything appears orange. If we wear glasses with purple lenses, everything looks purple. Likewise, if we wear an attitude of fear, everything scares us. If we wear an attitude of joy, everything delights us. Like our core beliefs, attitude is a power of the mind to view any event from one perspective or another.

Our attitude controls whether or not we're happy. It affects our thoughts, and our thoughts create our feelings—about ourselves and everything we experience. People with positive attitudes choose positive thoughts about situations and have positive experiences. People with negative attitudes choose negative thoughts about situations and have negative experiences. Your ability to choose your attitude in any life situation is your most powerful tool for creating both healthy self-esteem and a happy life.

On a hot, humid day, Diego and Jack were finishing a marathon. They'd been running for hours. Both were feeling the same degree of heat, exhaustion, and thirst; both were dripping with sweat and ready to drop.

As they crossed the finish line, they saw a glass half-filled with water on a table in front of them. Diego looked at the glass with a positive attitude and thought, Fantastic! Water! Just what I need! *There was a mile-wide grin on his face. He felt happy, thrilled, fortunate, and relieved.*

Jack looked at the same glass of water from a negative attitude and thought, Oh no! Only a half glass? I need a million glasses! This is awful! *Jack's face sank. He felt upset, angry, disappointed, cheated, and afraid.*

Both boys were in the same condition, both boys encountered the same situation, but they had completely different experiences.

It wasn't the situation that created their experiences; it was the thoughts created by their attitudes. Diego's positive attitude created positive thoughts, producing positive feelings, and he had a positive experience. Jack's negative attitude created negative thoughts, producing negative feelings, and he had a negative experience.

Your experience of life and your self-esteem are in your hands. The more you feed—or give energy and attention to—a positive attitude and positive thoughts, the more positive experiences you will have. The more you feed a positive attitude about yourself, the more positively you will experience yourself. This creates healthy self-esteem.

While this is a simple concept, it's not always easy to put into practice. There will always be times and circumstances when it's hard to choose positive thoughts. Someone could ask "What if

I see my house burning down? Am I supposed to have a positive attitude about that?" True, this would be a tough situation. However, we always have a choice. If we're watching our house on fire, we could think *Wow, I'm glad I'm out here, not in there!* or *I'm glad my family got out.* We could think *I'm glad my pets got out; I'm glad we've got insurance;* or *I'm glad the firefighters kept it from spreading.*

There are definitely times when working with attitude and thoughts is harder than others. But if we try, we have a chance of feeling better. If we don't try, we have no chance at all.

Attitude, to me, is more important than education, than the past, than money, than circumstances, than failures, than successes, than what other people say or do. It is more important than appearance, giftedness, or skill... The remarkable thing is that we have a choice every day regarding the attitude we will embrace for that day.

—Charles Swindoll

Explore

Explore the state of your own attitude by answering these questions on separate paper or in your journal.

- Would the following people describe your attitude as mostly negative or mostly positive?

  yourself

  your family

  your friends

  your teachers

103

someone you've just met

someone you're dating

Explain why.

- Explain how you developed your attitude toward life.

- As you go through each day, practice observing—without judgment—how your attitude affects your experiences of every situation.

- How has your attitude affected your self-esteem?

Become

If your attitude isn't as positive as you'd like, work on changing it by completing these exercises on separate paper or in your journal.

- Describe the positive attitude you would like to have.

- Tell how you would view these situations from a positive attitude:

    . It rains on the day of your pool party.

    . You lose the competition by one point.

    . You're picked last for the team.

    . The person you ask to a dance turns you down.

- As you go through the day, look for chances to work with your attitude. Whenever you notice yourself feeling negatively, observe your attitude—without judgment—and try making a change.

- Before you fall asleep at night, imagine yourself in a challenging situation. In as much detail as you can, picture yourself bringing a positive attitude to that experience. Visualize the positive results that unfold.

- Identify positive attitude choices you can make with friends, with family, and at school to build healthy self-esteem.

Affirm

I choose a positive attitude and create positive experiences.

The Power of Gratitude

Gratitude is an attitude of thankfulness and appreciation. People who live from gratitude put their attention on all that's good in their lives instead of what they don't like. They concentrate on what they have instead of what they think they're missing. They're even grateful for challenges, because they see them as opportunities to learn and grow.

Learn

We have a choice every day to focus on the conditions, people, and events that make us happy. We can feel grateful for the biggest to the smallest things: a friend, a home, a smile, our breath, fingers, phones, the sun, freedom. Gratitude increases joy, peace of mind, and the good in our lives. It centers us in the positive and highlights how much is already ours.

There are times when it's harder to feel grateful. When things don't go our way, when we're faced with loss, misfortune, or heartache, it's not as easy to pull our minds to the positive. But the choice is always there. Back behind the grief, there are still things to appreciate and there is always some good; we just have to remember it.

Focusing on what we're thankful for creates positive feelings. The more positive we feel, the more gratitude we have; the more gratitude we have, the better we feel. Gratitude increases positive thoughts about ourselves as well, building healthy self-esteem.

Molly and Will were in a support group for students whose parents were divorcing. Both had similar situations, but their experiences were different because of their attitudes. Both Molly and Will felt hurt and angry about their families breaking up. Will shared that every day he thought about what he'd lost. He believed his parents were cruel for putting him through this. He repeatedly remembered how things "used to be" and dwelled on missing his dad. He told himself that he'd been cheated and that his high school years were ruined. The more Will focused on what he didn't have, the worse he felt. His grades dropped, and he stopped going out with friends. He started hating himself and his life. His self-esteem declined. As Molly listened to the other kids, she realized she had a lot to be grateful for. Even though her dad had moved out, she stayed in the same house and school. She and her sister hadn't been split up, her dad lived close enough to visit often, and both her parents loved her. She still had friends, still played volleyball, still had her dreams of being a journalist. The more Molly thought about these things, the more she realized how fortunate she was, and she released her resentment. She even became grateful she now had more

time alone with her dad. Molly felt good about herself for mak-
ing it through a hard situation and coming out okay. She actu-
ally developed healthier self-esteem than when she had started.

When I started counting my blessings, my whole life turned around.

—Willie Nelson

Explore

Begin to discover the good in your life by completing the following exercises on separate paper or in your journal.

- Describe your life path of gratitude so far. Have you
  focused on how much you do have or how much you
  don't have? Tell why.

- What are the first three things you think of when
  asked what you are grateful for? Explain why these
  are at the top of your list.

- Name five things you are grateful for that:
  - are smaller than your hand
  - are larger than a chair
  - you cannot see
  - happened today

- Name five things about yourself you are grateful for.

- Describe what it was like to do the above exercises
  and focus on gratitude.

Become

Answering the following questions will help you develop a gratitude perspective. Use separate paper or write in your journal.

- Pay attention to the gifts of each moment in your life. Can you speak? Can you read? Do you love someone? Is there food in your home? For the next few days, keep a numbered list of anything you have to be grateful for. See how long it takes you to reach one hundred.

- Practice approaching challenges with gratitude. Identify things it's hard for you to be grateful for, and tell why. Then write new thoughts that might help you find gratitude for these things.

- Continue practicing gratitude for the next few weeks. Each morning, think of something to be thankful for. Each night, make your last thoughts those of gratitude. Write about how this affects you.

- Describe how your life will be different if you make gratitude your regular practice.

- Describe how your self-esteem will be affected if you focus on the good in yourself.

Affirm

I choose to focus on the good in my life.

The Power of Compassion

Compassion is a deep sympathy or caring for someone who is suffering and a desire to help that person. Suffering can come from anything from a stomachache to a death, a bad grade to a harsh word from a friend. It can be mental, emotional, physical, or spiritual.

Learn

When we feel or act on compassion for others or ourselves, we generate and expand the energy of loving-kindness in the world. We act with compassion more readily when we remember the core belief that every living creature has intrinsic value and worth, including ourselves. Recalling our equality to others, we feel more secure and act less defensively. This opens our hearts to embrace ourselves and others with benevolence and goodwill.

Compassionate statements sound like these:

- "Everything will be okay."

- "It doesn't matter; you're still my friend."

- "I'm so sorry this happened to you."

- "I'm not going to beat myself up over this."

- "I love you no matter what."

- "I'll help you."

Compassionate acts look like these:

- giving a hug to someone who's feeling sad

- visiting someone who is ill

- sitting with someone who feels anxious

- accepting yourself when you mess up

- bringing a stray animal in from the cold

- volunteering at a homeless shelter

Many of us are better at showing compassion to others than to ourselves. Sometimes we think that we don't deserve compassion or that others deserve it more. We may think we're being selfish if we care for ourselves. In reality, the more kindness we show ourselves, the healthier our self-esteem and the more we then have to give others.

We may think we don't know how to give compassion to ourselves. What would we do for a friend who is hurting? Give our time, attention and energy; sit and listen; ask what we could do to help? Those are the same ways to give compassion to ourselves. Give time, attention, and energy to our own needs. Respect our thoughts and feelings. Ask what we need, listen for our answers, and then act on them with kindness.

Treating ourselves with compassion helps us love and accept our authentic self unconditionally. Compassion feeds our positive thoughts and feelings toward ourselves and builds healthy self-esteem.

Jamar struggled with grades and had no patience with his mistakes. He told himself he was stupid and thought about quitting school. One day his math teacher asked Jamar to explain the syllabus to Luke, a new student. As Jamar went over it, Luke quickly became nervous and frustrated. He told Jamar that he struggled with math and this assignment list overwhelmed him. Jamar felt sorry for Luke and tried calming him down. He said the teacher was nice and would give him extra help. Jamar offered to share his notes with Luke, and Luke smiled for the first time. "You'd do better in class if you showed yourself the same compassion you show others," Mr. Walker said. "What do you mean?" asked Jamar. "You're so impatient and critical with yourself it makes you give up before you even try. Did you see how it helped Luke when you were kind and patient with him? Being kind and patient with yourself would help you do better in school."

If you want others to be happy, practice compassion. If you want to be happy, practice compassion.

—The Dalai Lama

Explore

Take a look at your own experiences with compassion by completing the following exercises on separate paper or in your journal:

- Describe a time in your life when you were struggling and wanted to be treated with compassion but weren't. Explain how that felt.

- Describe a time when you were struggling and someone did treat you with compassion. Tell what that felt like.

- Write about a situation where you showed someone compassion. How was this similar to or different from receiving it?

- Make a list of the things you do or say to others or yourself that express compassion.

Become

You can develop more positive relationships with both yourself and others by increasing your compassion. Complete the following exercises on separate paper or in your journal.

- Name two or more people you'd like to show compassion to. Describe what you would like to do or say.

- Describe a recent situation where you felt upset. Tell how you could have treated yourself with compassion.

- Identify areas where you could use more compassion with yourself. This could be in academics, socially, in family situations, or any area of your life where you are hard on yourself.

- Practice using compassionate self-talk and acting compassionately toward yourself as you go through the day. Describe what this feels like and how it affects your self-esteem. It may feel awkward at first if you're not used to treating yourself kindly. That's okay; be patient and give yourself compassion around this feeling!

Affirm

I choose to act with compassion toward myself and others.

The Power of Assertiveness

We feed relationships through the way we interact. Communicating in a positive way—using cooperation, compromise, and acceptance—creates positive relationships. Communicating in a negative way—using intimidation, blaming, and judgment—creates negative relationships.

Learn

There are three main communication styles: passive, aggressive, and assertive.

- A passive style conveys: "You count, but I don't." Passive statements sound like these:

  - "I wish I could go with them, but they probably wouldn't want me there."

  - "You go ahead. I'll just mess it up."

  - "I hate this TV show, but what can I do?"

- An aggressive style conveys: "I count, but you don't." Aggressive statements sound like these:

  - "I wish I could go with them, but they might not ask. I'll just show up; then they won't have a choice."

  - "Let me go first. I'll do it better than you could."

  - "There's no way I'm watching this show—give me the remote!"

- An assertive style conveys: "I count, and so do you." Assertive statements sound like these:

  - "I wish I could go with them; I'll ask if it's okay if I come along."

  - "Do you want to go first, or should I?"

  - "When this show is over, could we watch something we both like?"

Assertive communication is considered the healthiest because it's respectful to both parties. Assertiveness is based on the core belief that all human beings have intrinsic value and worth, including ourselves. When we act assertively, we stand up for our own rights and opinions and also respect the rights and opinions of others. When we act assertively, we respect our authentic self and feed the belief of equality. Acting assertively feeds positive thoughts about ourselves and creates healthy self-esteem.

Paige wants to borrow her sister's new sweater. She's afraid to ask because she's afraid her sister will say no. At dinner, Paige tells her sister how much she likes her new sweater. Her sister says thanks and continues her conversation. Then Paige slouches a little and says she doesn't feel well. She leaves the table and goes to her room. She lies on her bed and wishes her sister would offer to lend her the new sweater. She feels bad about herself because she never gets what she wants and thinks life isn't fair. Paige is acting passively.

Alexa wants to borrow her sister's new sweater. She's afraid to ask because she's afraid her sister will say no. Alexa goes into her sister's room when her sister is in the shower and takes the sweater from her drawer. She puts it on and puts another sweater over it so her sister won't see it. Later that night, when her sister sees Alexa come home wearing her sweater, she confronts her. Alexa says she found the sweater in her laundry basket and didn't realize it was her sister's. She yells at her sister, saying she should have lent it to her anyway. Alexa acts tough, but deep inside she feels bad about herself. She loves her sister and doesn't really want to hurt her.

Sophie wants to borrow her sister's new sweater. She's afraid to ask because she's afraid her sister will say no. Sophie decides it can't hurt to ask, so she approaches her sister. "I really love your new sweater. Would you mind if I borrow it sometime?" Her sister hesitates and then agrees. "I'm wearing it tomorrow, but you can borrow it next week. And then you have to wash it, okay?" Sophie agrees that's a fair request, and she wears the sweater on a date the following weekend. She feels good about herself because she and her sister worked out the situation cooperatively. She gains courage to act assertively again in the future.

The quality of your life is the quality of your communication.

—Anthony Robbins

Explore

The following exercises will help you understand your own communication style. Complete them on separate paper or in your journal:

- Over the next few days, take notes—without judgment—as to whether you act passively, aggressively, or assertively with different groups: siblings, parents, teachers, other authority figures, friends, and strangers (such as a restaurant server).

- Which style did you use most or least often? How did the person or situation affect your style?

- Describe the feelings you experienced when you communicated passively, aggressively, and assertively.

- How was your self-esteem affected when you used the different styles?

Become

Choosing assertive communication will improve both your relationships and your self-esteem. The following exercises will help you practice this style. Complete them on separate paper or in your journal.

- List the relationships or situations in your life where you'd like to act more assertively, and explain why.

- Choose one of the above, and practice assertiveness with visualization. Find a quiet place and sit comfortably. Take a few relaxing breaths. Release any tension you're holding in your body. Clear your mind. When you feel relaxed, close your eyes and imagine yourself with the people or in the situation you chose. Mentally go through the situation one step at a time, creating a positive story of what you would assertively say and do. Remind yourself of your equality to all others and their equality to you. Visualize yourself feeling calm and centered as you communicate assertively and act from your authentic self. Continue to breathe peacefully as you imagine this story unfolding scene by scene. In as much detail as possible, visualize how good you feel at the positive outcome of this interaction. Describe how this experience felt and how acting assertively affected your self-esteem.

- Over the next few days, continue observing your interactions and look for ways to act more assertively. As you feel comfortable, try making changes. Be patient with yourself; it's normal for this to take time and practice.

Affirm

I choose to act assertively, respecting both myself and others.

The Butterfly

One day, a man found a butterfly cocoon. He watched patiently as a tiny opening appeared in the cocoon, and then the butterfly struggled to force its body through the small hole. After a while, it seemed to stop making progress. It appeared as if it had gotten as far as it could and could go no farther.

The man decided to help the butterfly, so he used a pair of scissors to snip off the remaining bits of cocoon. The butterfly then emerged easily. But it had a swollen body and small, shriveled wings.

The man continued watching, expecting that at any moment the wings would enlarge and expand to support the butterfly's body, which would then contract. But neither happened! In fact, the butterfly spent the rest of its life crawling on the ground with a swollen body and shriveled wings. It never was able to fly.

What the man in his kindness and haste didn't understand was that the butterfly could fly only after it had struggled all the way through the opening. The restricting cocoon and the struggle out of it were nature's way of forcing fluid from the body into the wings, which would make it possible to fly.

Sometimes struggles are exactly what we need in life. If nature allowed us to go without obstacles, it would cripple us. We would not be as strong as we could have been. And we could never fly…

There Is a Reward in Every Struggle

Many people try to avoid experiencing anything unpleasant or uncomfortable. We believe life should go smoothly and easily, and when we face a hurdle we think, *What's wrong? This shouldn't be here!*

The longer we live, however, the more we discover that hurdles don't end. Once we cross one, there's another down the road. And finally we realize: Maybe there's a reason we have hurdles. Maybe there isn't anything wrong; maybe this is just the way the planet runs. Because no life is without struggle or challenge.

Once we embrace the existence of struggles, they lose some of their negativity. And when we learn to push through them, we find a reward waiting after each one—a silver lining in what first looked only like a dark cloud.

Coming to terms with struggles also brings the chance of feeling gratitude for them. In the middle of trauma, a lightbulb goes off. We stop complaining for a minute and think, *Wait, I remember—struggles help me grow. So I'm grateful for this chance to move forward. If I embrace this, I can learn from it, and I'll end up with a reward. Like the butterfly—the struggle gave it what it needed to fly.*

The following section describes four power-filled choices that are based on the principle "There is a reward in every struggle." They explain the benefits of choosing to meet our challenges instead of running from them. These choices might seem the harder ones at first, but the struggle always brings something better. And the experience of seeing it through increases our healthy self-esteem.

The Power of Managing Feelings

All human beings have feelings. And we have a right to all of them. But even though they're a natural part of life, we don't always know what to do with them.

Learn

Some people try to ignore, deny, or push away feelings. The problem is that stuffed-down feelings can reappear in negative ways. When we don't release them with care, feelings escape inappropriately. For example, holding in anger might cause us to lash out in rage; holding in grief might create stomach pain; holding in anxiety could cause a muscle twitch or a migraine.

When we experience a feeling, our brain releases chemicals—such as adrenaline—into our body, creating a physical reaction. We may notice our muscles tightening, light-headedness, stomach "butterflies," or other sensations. Because feelings have physical components, they can usually be released through physical activity. Three healthy activities that can work well are speaking, writing, and movement.

Speaking

Saying your feeling out loud, to yourself or someone else, can "take the wind out of its sails." Using an "I feel" statement will help; for example, "I feel so frustrated right now!" Or "I'm feeling really discouraged!" Or "I feel a little sad." This format lets you own your feelings (so that you're not blaming them on someone else) and release some of their charge. The stronger your feeling, the more energy can go into your statement.

Writing

Writing out your feelings, either longhand or electronically, also gives physical release. Moving a pen across paper or tapping letters on a keyboard discharges physical energy and dispels the chemicals released during feelings. You don't have to consider spelling, grammar, or other rules, because no one else has to read this. You can write whatever you want, without organization or even staying in the lines. The goal is simply to release emotion. When you're done, you can keep your writing or not. Sometimes the act of safely destroying it provides even more release.

Movement

Any physical movement can release tension and dissipate chemicals. This includes sports like basketball, baseball, gymnastics, running, swimming, or dance. It also includes stretching, yoga, walking, tai chi, karate, or deep breathing. Playing a musical instrument releases physical energy, as do drawing, painting, singing, and debate. Choose the activity that feels best for you at the moment. You may use a punching bag for anger, a yoga pose for anxiety, or sketching for loneliness. It's normal to vary your choices over time.

Bailey's health class was discussing depression and anxiety, two common feelings that become problems if they're not managed well. "But how do you manage feelings?" Bailey asked. "They seem overwhelming, and I don't know what to do with them. You can't just turn them off." "Good question," said Ms. Fitzgerald. "Feelings can seem overwhelming. Here's a healthy plan for managing them." She wrote on the board:

Observe

> *Name it: What is this feeling?*
>
> *Accept it: Every feeling is okay.*
>
> *Source it: What thought created this feeling?*

Act

> *Release it: In a safe way.*
>
> *Adjust it: Let go of or change the original thought.*
>
> *Use it: Let your feeling fuel a change.*

"Start by observing," she explained. "This brings perspective. First, name your feeling. Is it embarrassment? Disappointment? Joy? Next, accept it. Remember, all feelings are okay—it's how you express them that's appropriate or not. Judging raises anxiety, so accept whatever you feel. Then, source it—look for its origin. Find the thought that created it. Everyone is laughing at me *creates embarrassment;* This is the best day ever! *creates joy.*

"Now, decide how to act. First, release the feeling and the chemicals safely. Speak, write, draw, walk, run, shoot hoops, stomp your feet, sing, pound pillows, play tennis, or ride a bike. Next, adjust your feeling by working with the original thought. Either let it go from your mind, or consciously change it: from Everyone's laughing at me *to* It's not that bad, *or* Well, I could laugh with them! *Finally, use your feeling to fuel change. If you're angry because your phone malfunctioned, return it. If you're disappointed in your math grade, talk to your teacher."*

It feels good to express feelings appropriately, and it improves our relationships and increases our successes. Handling feelings well both releases them and creates healthy self-esteem. These are the rewards for managing feelings instead of denying them.

Trust yourself enough to know that you can feel anything and recover from it.

—Iyanla Vanzant

Explore

Take the first step to observe your feelings by completing these exercises on separate paper or in your journal:

- We usually recognize basic feelings: sad, mad, glad, and scared. But we experience many more over a day or a lifetime. Write down any of the ones listed below that sound familiar. Then describe a time when you felt this way.

abandoned	irritated
content	jealous
loving	peaceful
stressed	worried
shocked	angry
guilty	sad
excited	afraid
happy	betrayed
embarrassed	frustrated
confused	apprehensive
surprised	thrilled
brave	ashamed
disappointed	relieved
anxious	relaxed
lonely	depressed

- Over the next few days, pay attention to your feelings. We don't commonly do this, so be patient with yourself. Using the list above, or making your own, keep track of the feelings you experience and when. Then rate each feeling from 1 (low) to 10 (high) for how strong it was. Record this without judgment!

- Describe how you usually express strong feelings. Explain why you think these are healthy or unhealthy actions.

Become

Even if you've struggled in the past, you can practice managing feelings in healthy ways with these exercises. Complete them on separate paper or in your journal.

- List the feelings you experience most frequently, and number them in order from the easiest to the hardest to accept. Then practice writing or speaking accepting statements; for example, "It's okay to feel betrayed," or "I accept this feeling of loneliness," or "It's all right for me to feel relaxed." Know this is true—you have a right to all your feelings.

- List three feelings that seem unmanageable for you. Maybe you hide them, express them inappropriately, or just feel uncomfortable with them. Brainstorm healthy ways you could try releasing these feelings.

- Sit quietly and comfortably, and close your eyes. Take some relaxing breaths and release all tension. When you're ready, remember your feelings list and imagine yourself in situations where these feelings arise. Picture yourself recognizing your feeling, accepting it, understanding its origin, and deciding how to act. Try to stay relaxed, but if you sense tension, notice it without judgment, take a few breaths, and relax again. Show yourself compassion as you do this.

- Try putting one of your above ideas into action. If it works well, continue doing it. If not, try a different healthy way to manage the feeling. As you feel able, continue trying new ways to release feelings until you find those that work best for you.

- Record the rewards you realize when you manage your feelings in healthy ways.

Affirm

I accept my feelings and manage them in a healthy way.

The Power of Tolerating Discomfort

Discomfort is a general term for a feeling that can include many others. For example, Mateo felt discomfort when he was waiting to donate blood. More specifically, he felt scared and uneasy. Leah felt discomfort when she was on a first date. More specifically, she felt shy and intimidated. Caden felt discomfort when he was writing his oral presentation. More specifically, he felt nervous and worried.

Learn

It's normal to feel discomfort when we think, *Something's wrong.* This can be anything from stubbing our toe or dialing a wrong number to crashing our car or breaking up a relationship. Most people don't like discomfort and try to avoid it. Sometimes avoiding discomfort has positive outcomes, like when we take our hand off of a hot plate. Sometimes avoiding discomfort has negative outcomes, like when we skip class because we didn't study for a test.

In most situations, tolerating discomfort instead of avoiding it brings positive rewards. For example, when Mateo donated blood, he felt good about himself for helping others. When Leah stayed out with her date, she had fun and felt good about herself for sticking it out. When Caden gave his presentation, he passed the class and felt good about pushing through his fear.

Most discomfort can be transformed into something positive if we see the feeling through. When we tolerate discomfort, we move forward in life. This creates a double reward: (1) whatever we accomplish by sticking it out, and (2) the positive way we feel about ourselves, which builds healthy self-esteem.

Sam hated his literature class because he read slowly and was always behind. He never joined class discussions because he hadn't finished the chapter. When his mom suggested he go to a learning center, he rejected the idea. He couldn't think of anything worse than more reading. Finally his mom said he had to try. He went to one session and wanted to quit, but his mom wouldn't let him. After the second session, he talked with his tutor more and realized he liked her sense of humor. But he still hated reading. Sam went a third time, and the tutor commented on his improvements. "But I hate reading!" he complained. "You'll hate it less as you get better," the tutor said. Sam stuck out the semester and his lit grade improved. He noticed class wasn't as boring when he kept up with the reading. He even started enjoying some of the books. Sam finished the semester feeling good about himself. When he tolerated his discomfort, his grade went up, and he made a new friend in his tutor.

Kayla told her cousin Bria how angry she felt with her friend Nicole. "Nicole makes every decision about what we're doing, who's going, and when. She just plans without asking me, and then I have to agree or stay home." "Why don't you tell her how you feel?" asked Bria. "I'd feel awkward," Kayla said. "I'm not comfortable sharing those things." "Well, if you want to stay friends with Nicole, it'll be hard if you always feel ignored and angry." Kayla knew Bria was right. She decided to push through her discomfort and talk to Nicole. Nicole said she was sorry but she liked making all the plans and didn't want to compromise. Kayla was surprised and realized that Nicole wasn't the friend she'd thought she was. She also felt good about herself because she'd spoken up. She decided to spend more time with friends who were willing to hear her ideas.

Your struggles develop your strengths. When you go through hardships and decide not to surrender, that is strength.

—Arnold Schwarzenegger

Explore

You may be more able to tolerate discomfort than you realize. Complete these exercises on separate paper or in your journal.

- If you've done anything listed below, you've already pushed through discomfort and gained rewards. Write down the activities you've done, and add any others you can think of.

  learned to walk

  learned to talk

went to the dentist

talked to someone new

faced a fear

learned to share

helped a person in need

learned to read

admitted you were wrong

learned to ride a bike

learned to swim

tried a new activity

studied for a test

learned to write

woke up earlier than you'd like

- Describe the rewards you received from tolerating discomfort in the above situations. How would your life be different if you hadn't done these things? How did tolerating these discomforts affect your self-esteem?

- Name other people you know or have heard about who've tolerated discomfort and gained rewards. Describe their experience.

Become

Tolerating discomfort can feel easier when we focus on its rewards. Complete these exercises on separate paper or in your journal.

- Describe any of the following in your own life, and explain why they might cause discomfort. Then identify the rewards you'll gain if you tolerate the discomfort.

    - an upcoming life situation

    - current academic goals

    - current social goals

    - goals for yourself as an adult

- For each of the above situations, rate your degree of discomfort on a scale from 1 (low) to 10 (high). Then, on the same scale, rate the benefit of the rewards you'll gain. Write about what you observe.

- How will your self-esteem be affected if you tolerate these discomforts?

Affirm

I tolerate discomfort and reap the rewards of doing so.

The Power of Making Positive Decisions

We make hundreds of decisions every day, from what to wear to what homework to do first to what to say to our friend who is sad. Some decisions we think about carefully and some barely at all. Each decision has an outcome.

Learn

In general, positive decisions produce positive outcomes and negative decisions produce negative outcomes. For example, copying a paper from the Internet instead of writing your own is a negative decision that leads to a negative outcome: a failing grade, failing the class, or even suspension from school. Writing the paper yourself even if you struggle is a positive decision that brings a positive outcome: a grade you earned legitimately, avoiding punishment, and feeling good about yourself for completing a hard task.

A positive decision is usually one we know deep down is "right," morally or ethically. We know this choice will result in our highest good, and in the highest good for all.

In contrast, a negative decision is usually one we know deep down is not "right," morally or ethically. In the long run, it will hurt us more than help us and will likely hurt others, too.

Making positive decisions isn't always the easiest choice. In fact, many times it's the hardest. But once we make a positive decision, follow through on it, and experience the positive outcome, we rarely regret our choice. Likewise, while negative decisions can be tempting if they appear the easiest, once we get the negative outcomes, we regret making that choice. The discomfort we tried to avoid is far less than the discomfort of the negative outcome.

Daniel was working out at the health club when his friend Ben texted to see if Daniel could drive him to a party. Daniel knew his parents had let him have the car only to go work out. If he asked to drive Ben to a party, they would probably say no. But if he didn't ask and just went to the party for a little while, they wouldn't know. Daniel picked Ben up, and when they were almost at the party, the car started overheating and making knocking noises. Daniel didn't know what was wrong, so he had to call his dad to come get them. They were nowhere near the health club, and his dad knew Daniel had misused his car privilege. Daniel was grounded from driving the car for two weeks. He felt embarrassed for getting caught in a lie and guilty because he'd betrayed his parents' trust. "Think about your decisions more carefully," his dad said. "You knew it was the wrong thing to do. When you make a negative decision, there'll be a negative outcome." "But you wouldn't have let me go to the party," Daniel said. "You don't know that for sure," his dad answered. "Maybe we would have, or maybe we would've given you a ride ourselves. But asking first would have been a positive decision, and you would have gotten a positive outcome instead of losing the car and our trust."

When we push through the struggle and get positive outcomes from positive decisions, we get the benefit of our positive choice, and we feel good for taking this route. These rewards build healthy self-esteem.

It is our choices, Harry, that show who we truly are, far more than our abilities.

—Albus Dumbledore

Explore

Everyone has made both positive and negative decisions. Look at your own decision-making history by completing these exercises on separate paper or in your journal.

- List positive decisions you've already made that created positive outcomes; for example, doing homework when you didn't feel like it, doing extra chores to make money, not sharing a friend's secret even though you were tempted, or helping someone in need. Tell the rewards you gained from these decisions.

- Describe how making positive decisions in each of the above situations affected your self-esteem.

- Describe a situation where you made a negative decision and got a negative outcome. Explain why this created healthy or unhealthy self-esteem.

- Keep track of your positive and negative decisions this week. Describe what you observe.

Become

The following exercises will help you rehearse choosing positive decisions. Complete these exercises on separate paper or in your journal.

- Explain a positive and a negative decision you could make for each situation below. Describe the outcome for each, and tell whether it would create healthy self-esteem:

You said you'd go to the dance with someone, but you changed your mind. You don't know how to tell that person, so you consider just not being home when it's time for you to be picked up and then saying you forgot.

Your friend gave you money to buy cigarettes for her because you look older, even though you're both under the legal age. She said it would just be this one time. She reminded you she's done a lot of favors for you in the past.

Your coworker just cashed his last paycheck, and when he left for the night, he told you he'd quit and wouldn't be back to work. You were cleaning up after he left and found his cash in the employee break-room. You weren't close friends with him and don't know his phone number.

- Describe a situation you'll encounter soon where you'll have to make a positive or negative decision. Explain the outcome if you make the positive decision and why it's the right choice. Tell how this choice will contribute to your highest good, the good of others, or both. Then describe the outcome if you make the negative decision and explain why it is not a right decision. Tell how you or others would be hurt by this choice.

- Sit comfortably and quietly, take a few breaths, and clear your mind. Then visualize yourself confidently making the positive decision in the above situation.

Continue breathing deeply as you picture yourself reaping the rewards of this decision. Try to actually feel this positive outcome.

- Identify the times it feels hardest to make positive decisions, and list ways you could make it easier; for example, rehearsing ahead of time, listing the rewards of making the positive decision, or temporarily avoiding situations where you find it too hard to choose positive decisions until you feel more confident that you can.

Affirm

I choose to make positive decisions to create positive outcomes.

The Power of Taking Responsibility

Life brings many situations we don't want or don't like, from getting cold french fries or missing the bus to failing a class or feeling betrayed by a friend. When we're facing these situations, there are two ways to respond: we can take responsibility for our part in the situation, or we can blame other people or external circumstances for our unhappiness.

Learn

Blaming is often a first reaction. We want to find something outside ourselves to feel angry at. This feels more comfortable than thinking it's our fault and feeling angry at ourselves. We'd rather blame someone or something else so that we don't have to admit we did something "wrong."

However, when we choose to blame, we actually end up feeling worse about ourselves. When we blame, we give away our power and become victims. This creates more anger and bitterness. We feel helpless and trapped. Even though blaming initially seems easier than taking responsibility, it just brings false satisfaction and doesn't create healthy self-esteem. We don't grow or accomplish anything through blaming.

Blaming statements sound like these:

"I didn't get the lead in the play because the director doesn't like me."

"I was late because my brother didn't set the alarm."

"I couldn't get a job because my parents wouldn't drive me to the job fair."

"I tripped because you left your shoes in my way."

Statements of taking responsibility sound like these:

"I didn't get the lead in the play because the other person trying out had a better singing voice."

"I was late because I didn't check to see if the alarm was set."

"I couldn't get a job because I didn't try hard enough to find a ride to the job fair."

"I tripped because I didn't look where I was going."

When we choose to take responsibility, we empower ourselves. We put both our mistakes and our successes into our own hands. We gain the power to create our own happiness. And whatever the outcome, we can feel good about ourselves. We reap the rewards of developing our authentic self and creating healthy self-esteem.

Sierra got a low grade on her history test. She felt angry and disappointed. She told her parents she hadn't done well because the teacher hadn't provided a study guide. Then she felt helpless and angrier because she believed her grade was in the hands of someone who didn't care about her. She told herself life wasn't fair and she'd never succeed because teachers were all about themselves.

Amber got a low grade on her history test. She felt angry and disappointed. She wished the teacher had given out a study guide, but she realized that she could have asked the teacher directly what she should study. She decided to do that before the next test. She felt better about herself when she discovered there was a solution she could take charge of.

If you're a minor, it may seem like you really don't have much power in your own life. You're bound by the rules of your home, school, and community that limit the actions of persons under age eighteen or twenty-one. However, you can still take responsibility for your thoughts, feelings, and actions in response to those limits. You are still responsible for your own happiness and your own self-esteem.

Connor was an hour late past curfew. He didn't want to get in trouble, so he told his parents his ride had gotten sick and he'd had to find another way home. Later his parents found out he had lied, and they grounded him. "I wouldn't have to lie if you weren't so strict!" he said. He felt bad about himself because he told himself he had ridiculous, unfair parents and he'd be grounded the rest of his life because of them. He felt trapped and wished he were old enough to move out.

Jake was an hour late past curfew. He didn't want to get in trouble, but he knew if he lied the consequences would be worse. He apologized and said he'd lost track of time. His parents said he needed to find a way to get home on time, and if it happened again he'd be grounded. Jake decided to set the alarm on his phone to go off fifteen minutes before he had to be home. He tried it the next weekend, and it worked. He felt good about himself because he'd found a solution to the problem and had regained his parents' trust.

The willingness to accept responsibility for one's own life is the source from which self-respect springs.

—Joan Didion

Explore

Blaming may seem easier at first, but when we realize how it steals our power, it's not as appealing. Without judgment, explore your blaming history by completing these exercises on separate paper or in your journal.

- Describe times when you've blamed any of the following for situations you didn't like. Then tell what part you played in creating those situations.

your sibling(s)	the police
your town	local laws
authority figures	your friend(s)
your parent(s)	your intelligence level
your school	the weather
your teacher	your coach
your parents' income	the person you're dating

- Describe a current situation where you're blaming someone or something else for your unhappiness. Tell how blaming affects your control over your own life.

- Make a list of situations you currently feel unhappy about and some you feel happy about. Describe the part you play in either creating these situations or keeping yourself in them.

- Tell what happens to your self-esteem when you take responsibility for situations you don't like and for situations you do like.

Become

Think more about how blaming or taking responsibility affects your life by completing these exercises on separate paper or in your journal.

- Describe how you'd feel in the following situations if you (a) blamed someone else or (b) took responsibility for your thoughts, feelings, and actions. Which would create the healthiest self-esteem?

  You ask the student next to you for the answers during a test. The teacher sees you sharing information and calls you both up to her desk.

  You let your friend drive your parents' car even though they've told you not to. Your friend drives up on a high curb and damages a tire.

  You're at a party, and someone offers you alcohol even though you're underage. You accept the drink and then have another. The police show up at the party.

  Your friends spend almost the whole night talking with other people, because they say you're in a bad mood and they'd rather not be with you.

- Write about who you would like to hold the power for your happiness or unhappiness, and why.

- Explain any thoughts of discomfort you have about taking full responsibility for your thoughts, feelings, and behaviors.

- Write an intention for the kind of person you want to be. Do you want to feel good about yourself because of what you've actually accomplished or because you've blamed other people or circumstances for your troubles?

- Describe the rewards of taking responsibility for your life. How will these build healthy self-esteem?

Affirm

I keep my power by choosing to take responsibility for my actions.

The Donkey

One day a donkey fell down a well. The animal cried for hours as the farmer debated what to do. Finally he realized that the animal was old and the well needed to be covered up anyway, so it wasn't worth it to retrieve the donkey. He invited his neighbors to help, and they all began shoveling dirt into the well.

At first, the donkey cried horribly. Then, to everyone's surprise, he quieted down. A few shovelfuls later, the farmer looked down the well and was astonished at what he saw.

With every shovelful of dirt that hit his back, the donkey was doing something amazing. Every time the dirt fell, he'd shake it off and take a step up. Pretty soon everyone was stunned as the donkey stepped up over the edge of the well and trotted off!

Life is going to shovel dirt on you, all kinds of dirt. The trick to getting out of the well is to shake it off and take a step up. Every trouble is a stepping-stone. We can get out of the deepest wells just by not stopping, never giving up. Shake it off and take a step up.

I Am Not Limited by My Circumstances

As long as we're alive, we're going to fall into our own "wells." Some of them we'll see from a long way off, and others will take us completely by surprise.

As with everything else we're learning in this book, falling into a well can be handled in different ways. We can fall in and see only the problem, grumble about the depth and darkness and cold and damp and lack of air. We can moan and complain and use up our energy focusing on the limits of the situation. If we do this, there's a good chance we'll be stuck in the well forever.

Or we can choose to open our minds and see beyond the problem. We can take responsibility for falling in, see it as a challenge, and think about the rewards we'll reap from the struggle. We can look past the limits and see the possibilities. Instead of focusing on the cold, damp wall in front of us, we can look up and see the endless sky above. Like the donkey, we can choose not to let circumstances limit us.

The following section will describe four power-filled choices that are based on the principle "I am not limited by my circumstances." They will explain how no matter what happens around us, we can always draw on our inner resources to choose thoughts and behaviors that will produce something positive. Making this choice and finding success creates healthy self-esteem.

The Power of Possibility

It's so easy to believe we're stuck. Our first look at a situation gives us one view. We make a quick judgment and think we're trapped, with no way out. These thoughts bring up discouragement, help-lessness, or anger. But in reality we're rarely completely stuck, with no hope for change. Usually there are many possibilities we just haven't seen yet.

Learn

If you open your front door six inches, you can see a fraction of what's outside. Open it twelve inches, and your view doubles. Open it completely, and there's a whole world waiting—including paths across the ground and through the sky that can take you beyond what you can see. The wider the door is open, the more possibilities you realize.

The same is true in our lives. Focusing on just what's in front of us, we think we're limited. The wider we open our minds, the more our opportunities expand.

Stuck thoughts sound like these:

- *I want to go to college, but my parents can't afford it.*

- *I want to raise my grades, but I'm just not smart.*

- *I want some friends, but I don't know how to talk to people.*

- *I want to get a job, but I don't have any skills.*

Opened-mind thoughts sound like these:

- *I want to go to college. My parents can't afford it, but I can explore loans, grants, and scholarships, and I can get a summer job to help pay my way.*

- *I want to raise my grades. I struggle in school, but I can join a study group, ask the teacher for extra help, find a tutor, or learn new study skills.*

- *I want some friends. I don't know how to talk to people, but I could practice with my brother, read a book on social skills, or get tips from a counselor.*

- *I want to get a job. I don't have many skills, but I could take a class, start by volunteering, offer to work for less until I'm trained, or start in an entry-level position.*

We're limited only by our thoughts. When we see the infinite possibilities in every moment, situation, and person, we can grow, change, and become anything we desire.

Jonathan's family moved to a small town in his sophomore year. Jonathan hated it. He didn't like meeting new people. He liked cross-country, but the team was already chosen. He'd won regional competitions in chess club, but this school didn't have one. He wanted to get an after-school job, but the town was so small that there were few opportunities. The nearest bigger town was miles away, and Jonathan didn't drive yet. He felt lonely and bored and complained that his parents had stuck him in this awful place. Jonathan's older brother, Kyle, was home from college and was tired of his complaining. "You need to take

*off your blinders," he said. "You're making yourself miserable!"
"What blinders?" Jonathan asked. "This place is miserable—
there's nothing I like here." "Look beyond what you don't like,"
Kyle said. "See possibilities instead of limits." "What do you
mean?" said Jonathan. "I mean, there is always potential, but
you're stuck in your narrow view. Why don't you start a chess
club? Or play online—your computer links you to the world.
Go to the cross-country meets, get to know the team and the
coach, run on your own. If there are no jobs, get on a waiting
list—or start a lawn service, babysit, paint houses, or tutor. It
might feel like you're stuck, but you're restricted only by your
view. Open your mind and see the possibilities."*

You can take charge of your life. Look deeper; open wider.
Get out of the well. Know there are more answers than you can
imagine. You are not limited by your circumstances. When you
see and act on limitless possibilities, you transcend imaginary
limits, find successes, and create healthy self-esteem.

Imagination is more important than knowledge.

—Albert Einstein

Explore

You can work on seeing possibilities by first understanding
where you feel trapped. Complete the following exercises on separate paper or in your journal.

- Describe any ways you feel stuck in the areas below. Add more if you like.

academics	habits
relationships	emotions
family	physical body
hobbies	job
sports	social skills

- Explain any ways you feel trapped by the past and ways you feel trapped for the future.

- How does this stuck feeling affect your self-esteem?

- Describe a past situation where you felt stuck but got out of it. Explain how you found new options.

Become

You can train your brain to see beyond limits by practicing creative thinking. Complete the following exercises on separate paper or in your journal.

- See how many smaller words (for example, "due" and "rate") you can find in the larger word GRADUATED in five minutes. Take a break and try again. Then try again later.

- Make a list of new or nontraditional uses for each item below. These can be as logical or illogical as you like. For example, with a chair, you could stand on it, break it into firewood, or decorate it with ornaments.

chair	drum set
picture frame	car key
pair of socks	toothbrush
tennis racquet	golf ball
birdcage	drinking straw

- Name five common things you do on an average day, then identify a new way to do the same thing; for example, saying hey instead of hi, getting out of bed on a different side, sitting at a different place at lunch, walking a different way home.

- Look at your list of areas where you feel stuck. Consciously open your mind, and describe two or more ideas for change in each area.

Affirm

I can choose from limitless possibilities at every moment.

The Power of Conviction

Conviction is a strong belief and certitude. When we have conviction, we believe in ourselves and our ability to achieve our goals. We aren't discouraged by outside circumstances or other people. We accept roadblocks and detours without becoming disheartened or quitting. Conviction gives us the strength to handle challenges, follow our dreams, and stay true to our authentic self.

Learn

Without even realizing it, you had conviction as a small child. When you tried to walk but fell, you got back up. When you tried saying words but only babbled, you kept trying. When you mixed up the laces tying your shoes, you unwound them and did it again.

Your childhood conviction helped you achieve your goals. Do you have that same determination today? When you fall into "wells," do you keep trying until you get out? When you feel discouraged, do you refuse to give up? Using that childhood conviction in your present life will bring you successes and build healthy self-esteem.

Acting with conviction includes choices such as these:

- not giving up when things get tough

- believing we can do it

- refusing to let setbacks stop us from moving forward

- drawing on inner strength no matter what is happening outside us

- not wavering from our own truth despite differing opinions from others

Kalini knew she had a great concept and that her science project could work. But after reassembling and resetting it four times, she still couldn't get the robot to run right. Two of Kalini's class-mates said she should try another project. The teacher said she still had time to change. "I'm feeling so frustrated," she told them. "But I refuse to give up! I know this can work. Maybe I just need to come at it from a new angle." Kalini went for a walk to clear her mind. As she was walking through the park, the answer came to her. She went back to the lab, made the right adjustments, and her project won an award. She felt so glad she hadn't given up on her idea.

Valeria wanted to expand her school's recycling program. Tons of paper were discarded weekly, and soda cans overfilled the cafeteria bins. The Green Spirit Environmental Club had already committed to a tree-planting project. They sent her to the custodian, who sent her to the assistant principal. He said additional recycling costs were over their budget. Valeria felt discouraged but believed in her cause. She told her ideas to the PTO, and three adults offered to help. They researched costs of bins, paper recycling, and additional hours for collection and removal. Sometimes the project felt overwhelming, with road-blocks everywhere, but Valeria didn't give up. It took almost two years, but when she graduated, her school had a new recycling program, two other schools were using her ideas, and Valeria had earned a principal's award for community service.

Bringing conviction to any task will help you achieve your goals. It will also help you stand up to peer pressure, act assertively, and stay true to your authentic self, all of which build healthy self-esteem.

If you plan to build walls around me, know this—I will walk through them.

—Richelle E. Goodrich

Explore

The following exercises illustrate how most goals require some amount of conviction to reach. Complete them on separate paper or in your journal.

- Make a list of accomplishments you've achieved in your life. These can be anything from learning to add to painting your room to winning an award. Tell which needed the least and which needed the most conviction to achieve and why.

- Describe any challenges you've faced where you felt like giving up but didn't and were finally successful. Tell how it felt to accomplish your goal and how it affected your self-esteem.

- Interview someone older than you who has healthy self-esteem. Ask about times when this person acted with conviction to achieve his or her goals. Explain how this person's experience could motivate you.

Become

You can increase your inner strength and conviction with positive thoughts and practice. Complete the following activities on separate paper or in your journal.

- Copy down any of the following statements that sound good to you; then add your own. Write them in your assignment book, on your computer or phone, on sticky notes, or any place you'll see them. Repeat them until they become regular self-messages.

"I refuse to be discouraged."

"I believe in positive outcomes."

"I can do this."

"I will not give up."

"I believe in myself."

"I know I am capable of this."

"I'm not going to quit."

"I am strong enough to achieve this."

"I can see this through."

"Obstacles don't bother me."

- Last thing at night or first thing in the morning, lie still and feel the emotional and physical strength at the core of your body. Affirm your inner strength and conviction for meeting all challenges.

- List two personal goals and the potential obstacles that could deter you from meeting them. Describe how you'll face these obstacles with conviction. Write about how it will feel when you persevere and achieve your goal.

- Sit quietly and visualize yourself moving toward each goal you described. See yourself facing obstacles with courage and strength. Watch in detail as you act with conviction, overcome hurdles, and achieve your goal. Using your five senses, imagine the feeling when you accomplish this. Know you can make this vision a reality.

Affirm

I refuse to give up; I refuse to be discouraged!

The Power of Turning It Around

As we've already said, mistakes are normal, and when we accept and learn from them, we build healthy self-esteem. Some mistakes are bigger than others. Sometimes we regret things we've said or done for a long time after they've passed. Sometimes we think we've made so many mistakes or negative decisions we're stuck on a downward path and there's no turning back.

Learn

The belief that we're stuck is false and just moves us farther from happiness, success, and healthy self-esteem. The truth is, it's never too late to turn things around in some way. Turning things around means making a new choice, taking a new direction, getting out of the well we're in. It means rerouting our path, focusing on the good, and starting to build something new. It means looking at a challenging situation from a positive angle, opening our mind to possibilities, and believing we can achieve.

Turning things around can sound overwhelming, like more than we could manage. And sometimes we carry the false belief that we're so flawed there's no hope for change. But if these thoughts trip us up, it's simply time to look back at the three core beliefs and remember:

- Self-esteem comes from our thoughts, and we can work with those.

- Just like everyone else, we have value and worth—no matter what mistakes we've made.

- The way to our best self is by discovering and embracing our authentic self, not turning away from it.

Turning things around is possible. The beginning of change is simply one new thought, then one new feeling, and then one new action. No matter how old you are, how many mistakes you've made, or how many regrets you have, you always have the choice of turning things around. It may not be the easiest choice, but it's not impossible.

Hunter and Blake were riding in the backseat of Daniel's car. It was a warm night, the windows were open, and they had water balloons. They saw some kids they knew and threw the balloons, laughing when their friends got wet. Daniel drove back so that they could throw more. But this time another car got in the way, and the balloons hit the windshield, causing the driver to swerve and almost hit a tree. The driver called the police, who arrived in minutes. All three boys were taken to the police station, and their parents were notified. They had to appear in court and perform community service for three months. The judge spoke clearly: "Turn it around," she said. "Change this problem into an opportunity. Don't let these circumstances limit you." The boys worked as mentors to younger boys who were in trouble. Each of them spent six hours a week shooting hoops, riding bikes, getting haircuts, talking over lunches. Daniel, Hunter, and Blake soon realized the younger boys looked up to them, and they felt a responsibility to be positive role models. They put more energy and thought into their work. After three months, the judge said they'd gone a significant extra mile. She commended them and said the volunteer agency was offering them part-time jobs as activity leaders and junior counselors.

Ava believed she'd been in trouble her whole life. Her parents called her their "difficult" child. As a toddler, she "got into things," and as a teen, she was grounded repeatedly for making poor choices. Ava had shoplifted, taken her parents' car before she had a permit, and been caught smoking and suspended from school twice. Ava pretended she didn't care, but really she felt terrible. She didn't know why she made bad choices; she figured she was just a bad kid. Finally her parents took her to a counselor, Sarah Brennan. When Ava told Sarah how much she hated herself and her life, Sarah asked whether she'd like to change. Ava said, "Of course, but I can't. I'm just bad." Sarah told Ava no one is "just bad," no matter how many negative decisions they've made. She said Ava's past wouldn't limit her if she didn't let it; Sarah had helped kids in far worse situations turn their lives around. She gave Ava hope. They began working to change Ava's negative self-messages. Sarah taught Ava ways to relax and think before acting. As Ava started making positive decisions and getting positive outcomes, her mind opened to the possibility she could change. She realized she wasn't limited by her past. Over the next year, Ava turned her life around, and she began to like herself and the new life she was creating.

You are not limited by any circumstances. You can always choose to move in a new direction. Making this choice empowers you and creates healthy self-esteem.

Every day that you wake up, you get another chance to get it right.

—Tavis Smiley

Explore

Turning things around takes energy, but staying on a negative path makes things worse. Identify possible positive changes for yourself by completing these exercises on separate paper or in your journal.

- List any life situations you'd like to turn around, and explain why.

- Describe any habits you'd like to turn around. Tell how this would have a positive effect on your life.

- Explain how these situations and habits affect your self-esteem.

- Describe any way you'd like to turn your self-esteem around.

- Identify the thoughts and feelings that arise when you think about turning things around.

Become

Turning things around begins simply with our thoughts. Take the first step toward change by completing these exercises on separate paper or in your journal.

- Choose any items from your lists above and create plans for turning them around. List the steps you could take to make change happen.

- Describe how you could change your thoughts to accomplish your turnarounds. Write affirmations that would support you.

- Explain which of the three core beliefs would be helpful for making your turnarounds.

- Describe how you'll create healthy self-esteem by working on these changes.

Affirm

I can change negatives into positives.

The Power of Inner Peace

Anything we attempt is easier to achieve when we approach it from peace. When we're stressed, we bring tension to every relationship, experience, situation, and challenge. Starting from stress means we're tired and discouraged before we even begin.

When we're at peace, we bring peace to everything. Inner stillness helps us think clearly and make better choices. We're more patient with ourselves and others. We remember our healthy core beliefs and make positive decisions. Instead of meeting people and events with stress, we carry peace to every person and situation.

Learn

Many people think peace is something we have to "get," but actually we carry it within us. It's said that when the renowned artist Michelangelo was asked how he created the powerful statue of David from a solid piece of marble, he replied that he didn't: David was already in the stone. All he did was chip away the excess rock and unearth him.

Like David at the core of the stone, there is peace at our core. It might be covered up with negative thoughts, but if we chip away at them we'll find serenity underneath. When we center ourselves in that place, everything we say and do comes from peace. Whatever the outside circumstances, we can always reconnect with the tranquility deep within us. Five helpful pathways to that inner peace are explained here.

Breathwork

Focusing on our breath is a direct connection to peace. When we're tense, our breathing is rapid and shallow, reducing the oxygen flow to our muscles and brain. This increases anxiety and makes it hard to think clearly—and more likely we'll make negative decisions. We can access peace through our breath in these ways:

- *Taking one.* Remembering to take one conscious breath when we feel tension can bring us back to center and release stress from our bodies and minds.

- *Paying attention to it.* Focusing on inhalations and exhalations for a few minutes stills our mind and slows and deepens our breath.

- *Following it.* Paying attention—without judgment—to where our breath moves in and out of our body can help us relax.

- *Consciously deepening it.* Drawing our breath deeper into our lungs and abdomen relaxes our muscles and returns our heart rate to normal.

Logan was competing in the state gymnastics finals. He was up next and noticed his heart racing and jaw tightening. He felt slightly light-headed. Logan focused on his breath as his coach had taught him. Right away, it slowed and deepened. He took some deeper breaths and regained his stability. Despite the crowds, the judges, and the important task ahead, Logan found peace and brought it to his routine.

Thoughts

We've already discussed how thoughts affect feelings. Thoughts can create stress or serenity. Since they're always with us, they're a tool we can use at any time to access peace in these ways:

- *Observing them without judgment.* Just noticing the thoughts that are creating stress can separate us from them and remind us that we can change them.

- *Letting them go.* If thoughts create tension, we can notice that and make a conscious decision not to cling to them. We can choose to let them flow away without grasping on.

- *Changing them.* We can intentionally change thoughts that create tension to thoughts that create peace.

Deon was in the backseat of the car with his younger sister, Claire, as his family drove across the country on vacation. Deon told himself Claire was driving him crazy. She was constantly tapping her feet, making up songs, and asking him to play word games. There were three more hours to go until their next stop. He complained to his parents, but his dad just said, "Stop grumbling and change your attitude." The word "attitude" reminded him there was something he could control. He began substituting each stressful thought for a peaceful one. Instead of I wish I were home with my friends, *he thought,* I'm lucky to be on vacation. *Instead of* I wish she'd leave me alone, *he thought,* I'm glad she looks up to me and wants to interact. *Instead of* One more song and I'll go nuts, *he thought,* She's pretty creative, but maybe I'll listen to my music for a while, *and he pulled out his headphones. When Deon's thoughts changed, his feelings changed, and he felt peace instead of irritation.*

Mindfulness meditation

Mindfulness meditation was described earlier, when we discussed retraining our brain (principle 1). It is also an effective way to find peace. We can use it in these ways:

- *Practicing formally.* Meditating on a peaceful object or thought for up to twenty minutes lowers heart rate, reduces blood pressure, and releases tension. Focusing on peace grows peace. (See principle 1 for instructions.)

- *Practicing informally.* Most stress comes from focusing on the past or the future. Bringing our thoughts to the present moment—without judgment—any time during the day brings back our peace. (Again, see principle 1.)

- *Naming our actions.* We can move our focus away from stress and back to the present moment by affirming, silently or aloud, our current actions. For example, we may think or say *Eating, I am eating; Walking, I am walking; Showering, I am showering;* or *Smiling, I am smiling,* and so on. We can repeat these statements as many times as necessary to eliminate stressful thoughts.

- *Being aware of the present moment.* Stress usually comes from thoughts of the past or the future. When we notice this, we can bring our minds back to the present moment. Observing with our five senses the sights, smells, textures, sounds, and tastes of only what is here and now takes our thoughts away from stress and back to peace.

Tori is trying to watch a movie, but her mind keeps wandering to her oral surgery appointment. She tells herself getting her wisdom teeth out might hurt, which creates tension and fear. She tells herself her mouth might be swollen for days, which creates anxiety and embarrassment. Then Tori tells herself she's dumb for worrying, and this creates frustration and impatience. Finally, Tori remembers mindfulness. She notices her thoughts without judgment and brings them back to the present. She thinks, Watching a movie, I am watching a movie. *Then she notices the softness of the couch, the warmth of her sweater, the music playing and the plot of the movie. She lets go of the thoughts of surgery and feels peace.*

Belief in a higher power

Many people believe in a power greater than themselves. This belief helps them make sense of life, the universe, and all that goes on in it. Most faith traditions, even though they're different in other ways, are based on this belief. Believing in a higher power can help us find peace in ways like these:

- *Aligning with a greater peace.* Affirming that there is a power stronger than any situation centers us in a peace bigger than our own. We can find this by going to places we feel this power, such as places in nature, a place of worship, a quiet room, or within ourselves.

- *Finding a reason for things.* Believing in a purpose for life and all its experiences helps us release thoughts of fear and regain peace when we're faced with struggles. When we trust there is a reason for everything that happens, it helps us accept the difficult times because we believe they have a purpose.

- *Asking for help.* Seeking guidance, strength, or wisdom from a source that's wiser and more powerful than ourselves can help us feel more secure. We don't think we're facing our challenge alone.

Ella always wanted to be a police officer like her mom. It was her childhood dream, and she couldn't wait until she could join her mom in this field, hopefully on the same force. Then one day Ella learned she was color-blind to an extent that she wouldn't qualify to work on the police force. At first she was devastated, feeling both angry and sad. Her mom said, "I'm disappointed, too, Ella. But things happen for a reason. Maybe there's something else you're meant to do. Let yourself grieve this loss, but then let it go and listen for guidance. Don't let circumstances limit you." Ella knew her mom was right; she'd experienced this before. When she remembered her belief in the wisdom of a higher power, she felt more peaceful. She believed an even better opportunity would come along for her.

Acceptance

Our first thoughts when facing hard situations are often something like *This shouldn't be happening!* or *It shouldn't be this way!* We actually fight with reality.

It's normal to feel upset when we don't like what's going on in our life. But rejecting it doesn't change it. We can go around for days feeling angry or sad, and wishing things were different. But all that does is make us feel awful; it doesn't make things better and it doesn't bring us peace.

164

When we choose acceptance, we can release some stress. Acceptance doesn't mean we like what's happening or that we aren't going to work for change. It does mean we stop fighting reality. For example, if we find out our dad took a job in another state and we have to move and leave all our friends, we can think our life is terrible, feel miserable, hold a grudge, slam doors, and isolate ourselves. This doesn't change reality, but it does keep us miserable. Or, we can accept what's happened, find peace, and work from there. Maybe we'll plan great last parties with our friends and visits over school breaks, or explore the new place we're going. Acceptance helps us face life with peace instead of stress.

> *Maggie's family dog, Rocky, wasn't doing well. He was a year older than Maggie, and she hadn't known life without him. Maggie felt such loss and sadness; she didn't want to lose Rocky. She began having trouble concentrating in school and didn't have any appetite. "We're all feeling sad," Maggie's dad said. "Rocky's been our friend for so long. But we need to accept that his time with us is ending. This is the way life is set up. Let's fill his last days with love." Maggie tried reminding herself that she couldn't change this and falling apart wasn't helping Rocky. So she cuddled with him on his favorite blanket, gave him his favorite treats, and petted him until he fell asleep. She didn't like what was happening, but accepting it helped her act from peace instead of stress.*

All the principles in this book will be easier to practice if you come to them from peace. You'll find your own best ways to access that peace. You can try the suggestions here or discover your own—as long as you find safe, healthy ways to release drama or high emotion and return to peace. Staying grounded in peace empowers you, increases your successes, and builds healthy self-esteem.

Each one has to find his peace from within. And peace to be real must be unaffected by outside circumstances.

—Mahatma Gandhi

Explore

Consider the benefits of peace, and explore your own ideas by completing these exercises on separate paper or in your journal.

- Identify the circumstances and people with whom you feel the most stress and those where you feel most peaceful. What thoughts create your stress or peace in these situations and with these people?

- Describe what would happen if you brought peace or stress to the following situations:

  Your teacher announces an unscheduled quiz.

  Your best friend gets hurt playing volleyball and asks you to ride in the ambulance with her.

  The person you're dating says you need to have a serious talk.

  You're babysitting two toddlers, and there are tornado warnings for your town.

  Your brother accuses you of lying to him, and you didn't.

- People describe higher power in many different ways:

spirit	source
life	soul
peace	divinity
love	holiness
nature	miracles
God	gratitude
energy	faith
eternity	heart

Write down the words that make sense to you, and add your own. Explain anything you believe about a higher power.

Become

Practice accessing and increasing your peace as you complete these exercises. Use separate paper or write in your journal.

- Try any of the breathwork, thinking, or mindfulness exercises explained above. Tell which ones work best for you and how you could use them in your daily life.

- These words can be helpful to repeat when you need to find acceptance: "Grant me the serenity to accept the things I cannot change, the courage to change the things I can, and the wisdom to know the difference." If these lines don't work for you, try writing your own.

- Describe how you could use your belief in a higher power to access peace.

- Sit quietly and comfortably and close your eyes. Take a few slow, deep breaths. Imagine you're in the most beautiful, peaceful place you can imagine. This can be real or a place you make up. Look around at the colors, shapes, and textures. Notice that everything brings a sense of peace. Notice that all the sounds, smells, and tastes are harmonious. Notice that anything you touch feels pleasing. Release any tension you're holding in your body. Let every cell relax into the beauty and tranquility of this place. Imagine a warm, golden light flowing around and through you, bringing deep peace to your body, mind, and spirit. Focus on this feeling for a few minutes or as long as you're comfortable. Know that bringing this peace into the rest of your life will help you create successes and healthy self-esteem no matter what circumstances you face.

Affirm

I center myself in peace.

Ending Note

You may be at the end of this book, but you're also at a beginning—you're moving forward with new ideas. By having read any part of this book, you've done something positive for yourself, which builds healthy self-esteem. And you've got new information about how to create the life you want.

What you've read here will be added to what you already know. You may consciously try some new thoughts and behaviors because you think they could work for you. You may notice you're thinking from a new viewpoint without even trying. Some ideas you've learned will work well, and some may not. Some may feel easy to put into practice, and some may feel very challenging.

Many teens decide to work with an adviser or counselor to help them push through personal roadblocks. This may be right for you or not. You may want to read more books on self-esteem or anything else that helps you grow. Trust your inner wisdom to guide you.

Wherever you go from here will be unique to your individual journey. But whatever your next step, know that you carry with you the power to create the self-esteem and the life you want. Your thoughts determine your experience of life. Keep feeding the positive! Your self-esteem is in your hands.

Acknowledgments

I would like to thank Tesilya Hanauer for bringing me great opportunities, sharing the creative process so richly, and guiding my ideas with care; Karen Schader for her easy yet professional way, for her respect of my work, and for keeping it fun; Amy Blue, Research Librarian Extraordinaire, for going the extra thousand miles and finding needles in haystacks; and the entire New Harbinger staff, whose knowledge, skill, kindness, and patience bring warmth, sanity, and joy to each project.

Lisa M. Schab, LCSW, is a licensed clinical social worker with a private counseling practice in the greater Chicago, IL, area. She has authored fifteen self-help books and workbooks for children, teens, and adults, including *The Anxiety Workbook for Teens, The Self-Esteem Workbook for Teens,* and *Beyond the Blues.* Schab teaches self-help workshops for the general public, conducts training seminars for professionals, and is a member of the National Association of Social Workers (NASW). You can find out more about Schab at www.lisamschabooks.com.

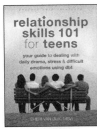
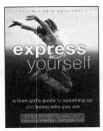